OTHER BOOKS IN THE *IRISH REVOLUTIONARIES* SERIES:

TOM BARRY: IRA FREEDOM FIGHTER

LIAM LYNCH: THE REAL CHIEF (FORTHCOMING)

DAN BREEN AND THE IRA (FORTHCOMING)

SEÁN TREACY AND THE TAN WAR (FORTHCOMING)

9/2286057

ÉAMONN CEANNT

Supreme Sacrifice

WILLIAM HENRY

Foreword by Éamon Ó Cuív

MERCIER PRESS
IRISH PUBLISHER – IRISH STORY

MERCIER PRESS

Cork

www.mercierpress.ie

First published in 2005 under the title *Supreme Sacrifice*.
This edition published in 2012.

© Text: William Henry, 2005, 2012

© Foreword: Éamon Ó Cuív, 2005, 2012

ISBN: 978 1 85635 956 6

10 9 8 7 6 5 4 3 2 1

A CIP record for this title is available from the British Library

Printed and bound in the EU.

Contents

Acknowledgements		9
Foreword		13
Introduction		19
1	The Rise of Nationalism	21
2	From Birth to Manhood	26
3	Contribution to the Gaelic Revival	33
4	Falling in Love	41
5	Path to Rebellion	48
6	Foundation of the Irish Volunteers	56
7	Gun-Running	61
8	Planning for Rebellion	66
9	Holy Week	78
10	Mobilisation	84
11	A Terrible Beauty is Born	97
12	Securing the Union	105
13	Attack on the Union	112
14	Calm before the Storm	123
15	Final Assault	129
16	The Galway Rebellion	135
17	Surrender	140

18	Court Martial	151
19	Execution	163
20	Aftermath	180
Epilogue		188
Notes		192
Bibliography		210
Index		215

In memory of a wonderful lady
Joan Gallagher
(1949–2003)

1798 Rebellion poster. Published by John Arigho, Christchurch Place, Dublin; printed by James Walker & Company, James's Rd, Dublin (*courtesy of the O'Brien collection*).

Acknowledgements

I wish to thank the following people without whose help and support this work would have been an extremely difficult task. Very special thanks to my wife, Noreen, and our children, Patrick, David and Lisa, for their patience, understanding and support over the past ten years.

I owe a great debt of gratitude to the late Joan Gallagher, granddaughter of Michael Kent (brother of Éamonn Ceannt). This book would not exist without her tremendous support. She secured access to the private family manuscripts of Áine Ceannt, the Lily O'Brennan documents and many more sources and photographs. This project took many years to complete and I truly appreciated her great patience. Sadly, Joan passed away just prior to the completion of the book and it is therefore appropriate that it should be dedicated to her memory.

Thanks also to Joan's two sisters, Mary and Nora Gallagher, who were extremely helpful and supportive throughout this project; Éamon Ó Cuív for his support during the project; Mary Hession and Tom Small who translated much of the Irish language documents; John and Mary O'Toole; Martin and Angela Carr; Dennis and Nancy Foley and their daughter, Anne, for their hospitality while I was working in Dublin and Celbridge; Noelle Dowling and her team in the Allen Library for cataloguing the required material.

Others who gave support include Professor Timothy O'Neill, Fr Tommy Murphy, Brigadier-General Patrick O'Sullivan, Aran O'Reilly, Br Christy O'Carroll, Cecilia Travers, John O'Donnell, Marie Mannion, Pat Hawes, Maureen Moran, Mary Qualter, Mary Kavanagh, Br Thomas Connolly, Derek and Geraldine O'Hehir, Jim Herlihy, Garda Donal Kivlehan, Mary Small, Sheila O'Donnellan, Una Cannon, Councillor Martin Quinn, Marie Silke, Ryan Tubridy, Maeve Doyle, Pat Rooney, Ann Mitchell, Bernie Finan, Rosie Dunne, Gerard Thornton, Gerry Darcy, Mike Faherty, Mary O'Leary, Kieran Hoare, Monica Coughlan, Mick Killeen, Mike O'Connor, Margaret Hughes, Brigid Clesham, Liam Frehan, Marie Boran, David M. Ceannt, Michael McDonagh, Margaret Murphy, Pat McGlynn, Tom Kelly, Martin Gargiulo, Jackie Uí Chionna, Bill Scanlan, Tom Kenny, Desmond Kenny, Rena Lohan, Bridie Kineevy, Liam McNulty, Michael O'Connor, Joe Burke, Reggie Darling, Maura Flaherty, Paul Flaherty, Anne Maria Curley, Michael McDermott, Dr Noel Kissane, Dónal Ó Luanaigh, Sinead McCoole, Tom Desmond, Niamh O'Sullivan, Assumpta Ward, Donal McCoy, Eugene Halferty, Gerard Lyne, Elizabeth Kirwan, Paddy O'Donnell, Joe Howley, Joe O'Shaughnessy, Pat Cooke, Olivia McCormack, Frances Kinneen, Kitty Lardner, Tom Flynn, Gerry Glynn,

Miles McHugh, Fergal O'Connell, Laura Walsh, Una McMahon, Christopher Townley, Phonsie Harty, Andy Feeney, Aonghus Ó hAonghus, Brian Crowley, Paul Duffy, Lorcan Collins and the late Joe O'Halloran.

Thanks to the council of trustees of The National Library of Ireland, Dublin; The National Museum of Ireland, Dublin; James Hardiman Library, National University of Ireland, Galway; The Civic Museum, Dublin; Dublin City Council; Dublin City Archives; Kilmainham Gaol Museum, Dublin; Galway County Library, Island House; Norman Morgan Library, Loughrea; The Allen Library, Dublin; North Richmond Street Christian Brothers School, Dublin; Ceannt Barracks Officers Mess, Curragh, Kildare; Dublin Pipers Club; Fountain Resource Group, Dublin; Radio Telefís Éireann, Dublin; Dúchas – The Heritage Service; St James's Hospital Board, Dublin; St James's Hospital Archives, Dublin; the *Irish Independent*; *The Times*; *The Irish Times*, *The Freeman's Journal*; St Columba's Credit Union and Committee, Mervue, Galway; Iarnród Éireann and Management, Galway; Great Southern Hotel and Management, Galway.

I am deeply indebted to all of the following people: Maeve Frost, Tommy Joe Furey and Professor Davis Coakley for their support and the use of their photographic collections; Robert Waller, for all his help in the reproduction of photographs; Alderman Michael Leahy for his enormous support throughout this project. Special thanks to Jacqueline O'Brien for all her support and the many hours spent researching and proofreading this book. Special thanks also to Anne Maria Furey, Marita Silke, Caroline Goonan, Noreen Henry, Jim Higgins, Tim Collins, James Casserly and Liam Curley for proofreading and for making many valuable suggestions.

None of the above-mentioned are in any way responsible for the opinions expressed, or conclusions arrived at, in this account of the life and posthumous reputation of Éamonn Ceannt. For this I alone am responsible. Without the support and help of all of these people, this book would not exist in its present form. In my opinion, friends are one of the most important commodities in life and I thank God for all the wonderful friendships extended to me.

Foreword

There has been much talk in recent years about what would have happened in Irish history if 1916 hadn't taken place. In this context I think it is appropriate to quote the words of Seán Moylan from his memoir of the Irish War of Independence, in which he says, 'But, in considering the evil a man does and the mistakes he makes, one's judgement is less likely to err when the man is placed against the background of his time and country. The intransigent who, when his country was invaded and overrun during the latest Great War, took arms against the invader and in secret, and in civilian guise, killed, burned and destroyed the forces and the equipment of the invader, is lauded as a hero – in Poland *tuigeann tú* – but here in Ireland every man who took up a gun and, with the dice completely loaded against him, went out to fight for his country's liberty in the only fashion possible, was deemed a murderer by those who controlled all the organs of publicity.'

This demand for recognition of their rights as men has been the real source of revolt in Ireland. It is in complete opposition to the dialectics of the Marxist materialist and, even though the demand for economic rights has been interlocked with it, always the driving force has been 'wrested from the things of the spirit'. Thus, in judging the events of 1916 and what led up to them, one should not judge them in the context of the era of the Good Friday Agreement, or of open negotiation between an elected Irish government and the British government, or of the era of all-Ireland referenda.

If 1916 had not taken place it is likely that after a long delay Ireland could have been granted home rule. However, the whole nature of home rule would have led to a very different Ireland than the one we enjoy today. Home rule was about a limited form of self-rule within the Empire. It was about regional government without the powers of external affairs and an army. It was about a country without the right to make its own decisions in international affairs and the right to sit at the table of nations. It would have been impossible for us to make our own independent decisions during the Second World War.

The other great context in which 1916 must be judged is the context of the choices as they were seen at the time. The vast majority of people in that era did not question the fundamental question of war itself and for most the issue was: did you fight for Ireland in Flanders, or if there was fighting to be done, did you make your stand at home? Thus, to judge the acceptability of 1916 without judging the morality of the First World War is to take history, as Seán Moylan so aptly put it, out of the context of 'time and country'.

By any measure the 1916 Rising was a most extraordinary affair, not least because of its success and the incredible personalities who led the Rising: people of culture, idealism and education. The extraordinary conduct of the Volunteers ensured that after the executions the sympathy of the Irish people would be with them. In recent years, the leaders of 1916 have often been maligned as being bloodthirsty militarists. Nothing could be further from the truth.

The words of Pearse's surrender on 29 April 1916 indicate the real nature of these leaders. In his surrender he said, 'In order to prevent the further slaughter of Dublin citizens, and in the hope of saving the lives of our followers, now surrounded and hopelessly outnumbered, the members of the Provisional Government present at Headquarters have agreed to an unconditional surrender, and the Commandants of the various districts in the City and Country will order their commands to lay down arms.'

So who were these men who have been demonised on the one hand and held up as icons on the other in the time since their heroic and tragic deaths? To a lot of people the names of 1916 leaders are simply that, names written in books on the Proclamation, pictures on the walls in Dublin Castle or busts in the lobby in Dáil Éireann. Very little is known by the public about their background, their motivations, their history, their families, etc. This is a great pity, as they were people of great character, who have left us an incredible legacy.

We are in William Henry's debt for providing us with a biography for the first time of Éamonn Ceannt, one of the most interesting, if little known, of the 1916 leaders. It is interesting that as a child, my grandmother, Sinéad de Valera, often mentioned Éamonn Ceannt when talking about the leaders of 1916. She, of course, knew most of the leaders of 1916 through her involvement with the Gaelic League and gave to us a very human account of them. Unfortunately, like most young people, we did not listen carefully enough and a lot of what she said is now forgotten. However, I can testify to the fact that this man made a great impression on her and, having read William Henry's book, I can understand why.

Éamonn Ceannt was born in County Galway, where his father, James, was a member of the Royal Irish Constabulary (RIC). He moved with his family to Ardee in County Louth when Éamonn was only two years of age. This book portrays Éamonn as a lively, enthusiastic and committed person, with an incredible love for his country, and for its culture.

One of the things that always fascinated me growing up was the fact that a large number of the 1916 leaders were family men who made the decision to fight in 1916 in the nearly certain knowledge that they would be killed or executed. I can remember one of my brothers or sisters asking my grandmother what she thought when Éamon de Valera, her husband, said that he was going out to fight in 1916. At that time she had four children and was expecting her fifth. With all the determination she could muster she said, 'If he had not gone out, I would have sent him, because I was in it first.' This was not to make little of the huge consequences for her and the family if he had been killed or executed, but to show the huge commitment that she shared in relation to the need for a stand to be made for Irish freedom. A very interesting and similar pattern emerges from the life of Éamonn Ceannt. The incredible relationship with his wife Áine and the fact that he left a son, Rónán, must have made parting absolutely horrendous, but what also shines through is her commitment to their shared cause. This, in my view, reinforces the point that at that time they believed, with fair justification, that there was no other way to achieve the freedom of this country.

Nearly a hundred years on, we enjoy the benefits of their supreme sacrifice. Our country is recognised from one end of the globe to the other. The part of Ireland that won its independence has had virtually uninterrupted peace since 1923.

Since the Good Friday Agreement, for the first time the political arrangements of this country have been put in place by the free vote of the Irish people, north and south, acting by agreement.

Irish games and Irish music have never been stronger and the Irish language, despite the prophets of doom, is thriving in all parts of the country. Although no country is perfect, I am happy that if he were alive today, Éamonn Ceannt would feel that the dreams he had in 1916 have been far exceeded by the achievements since.

There is sometimes a belief that the leaders of 1916

lived in some detached world of idealism. Yes, they were idealists, but they were idealists who lived, laughed and cried in the same type of world that we live in with all its imperfections.

In this context, William Henry's book clearly shows Éamonn Ceannt, and all of the other people involved in the Rising, as they actually were: people of their time, striving to do the best for their country.

Éamon Ó Cuív, TD

Introduction

Irish history tells the story of many men and women who fought and died for the freedom of their country. Since the Anglo-Norman invasion of Ireland in 1169, there has been resistance of one type or another to foreign rule. The first chapter of this book contains a brief background of Irish history from 1690 to 1890. Some of the most prominent figures of modern Irish history are, of course, the leaders of the 1916 Easter rebellion and among them is Éamonn Ceannt, about whom very little has ever been written. However, when one looks more closely at his life, one sees the emergence of a man equal in status to Robert Emmet and Theobald Wolfe Tone.

Some years ago, James Casserly, editor of *St Patrick's Parish Magazine* asked me to write an article about Éamonn Ceannt. Shortly after its publication a number of people contacted me requesting more information about Ceannt and so I began work on this book. At first Éamonn Ceannt seemed to be the most elusive of the rebellion leaders, but, through intensive research over the past number of years, an extremely clear picture has emerged of a dedicated and determined figure, whose love for his country was equalled only by his love for his family.

He was born into an environment which one would not readily associate with republicanism, but as a young man he became very involved in, and quickly moved through the ranks of, movements such as the Irish Republican Brotherhood (IRB) and the Irish Volunteers. He strongly believed in the ideals of Wolfe Tone and, like Tone, he paid the ultimate price for those beliefs.

1

The Rise of Nationalism

The defeat of the Jacobite forces at the Battle of Aughrim on 12 July 1691 signalled the end of any hope of an Irish victory in the Jacobite/Williamite war. Limerick, the last stronghold of the Irish, surrendered on 3 October, thus ending the war. Under the terms of surrender, Irish soldiers were allowed to leave Ireland with their commander, Patrick Sarsfield. About 12,000 followed Sarsfield to France in an exodus which became known as the 'Flight of the Wild Geese'. The Jacobite/Williamite war signalled the end of major field battles in Ireland and from 1691 until the signing of the Anglo-Irish Treaty in December 1921, warfare in Ireland was mainly based on rebellion and guerrilla tactics. The war had cost Ireland dearly, leaving the country devastated, with an estimated 25,000 Irish soldiers killed in the conflict and many more, both civilian and military, dying from disease and famine. The writer Seán Ó Faoláin, described the tragedy as 'all but the end of a race'.[1]

During the 1690s the Penal Laws were introd

9/2286057

which deprived Catholics of many civil rights, including education and religious freedom. These laws also deprived Ireland of a powerful political force in its Catholic nobility, clearing the path for the rise of the Protestant Ascendancy to power, and the oppressive landlord system associated with that time. This system eventually caused terrible unrest and helped create many revolutionary figures. The rebellion of 1798 led to the arrest and death of Theobald Wolfe Tone. At his trial he was sentenced to death by hanging. However, in the early hours of 12 November 1798 he cut his own throat, using a razor apparently left behind by his brother, Matthew, who had been hanged earlier for his part in the rebellion. Tone lingered until 19 November when he died. Some say the act was suicide, while others believe that he simply chose the manner in which to die. Tone had helped to establish the Society of United Irishmen in 1791 and later became its most celebrated member; he is renowned as the 'Father of Irish Republicanism'. The failed rebellion of 1803 led to the public execution of Robert Emmet in Thomas Street. Many years later, these self-sacrifices clearly had an influence on Ceannt who regularly visited Tone's grave in the churchyard at Bodenstown, County Kildare.[2]

England, in securing her grip on Ireland, abolished the Irish parliament and on 1 January 1801 introduced the Act of Union, which meant that the parliament at Westminster would now legislate for Britain and Ireland. Initially the union had been described as a marriage between both countries and it seemed at first that Ireland had everything to gain with plans for major investment in the country. However, over time, the reality proved very different and, with English investment not forthcoming, Irish industry collapsed, causing widespread unemployment. Catholic emancipation, which was expected to follow the union immediately, was not granted until 1829, and only then after a desperate struggle. Ireland continued to seek a repeal of the union and by 1843 the demand was so strong that the British parliament could no longer ignore the situation. The driving force behind the repeal movement was Daniel O'Connell. He and his followers were pledged to obtain repeal only by legal and constitutional means. At first the movement was hugely successful, with tens of thousands of people turning out to attend the so-called 'monster meetings'. However, the enthusiasm of the repeal movement was crushed after O'Connell called off what was supposed to be his greatest of all gatherings, at the ancient Irish battleground at Clontarf, County Dublin. It had been planned for Sunday 8 October 1843, but the government, fearing a rebellion, banned the meeting with the threat of military activity.[3]

Another major contribution to unrest in Ireland was the devastation caused by the Great Famine of 1845–47, which left some million and a half dead; the true figure will never be known. At least another million people fled to other countries during one of the most tragic events in Irish history: this had far-reaching effects on Irish nationalists. Even during the famine, rebellion emerged through the Fenian movement and although the rebellions were total failures, they did manage to keep a spark of hope burning through those long dark years. In the aftermath of the famine, the eviction of tenant farmers was rampant and by 1870, only three per cent of Irish householders owned the land they occupied. This led to land agitation and the foundation of the Irish National Land League. One of its founders, Michael Davitt, was himself a victim of the evictions. By the late nineteenth century the landlord system had taken its toll in Ireland. In 1886 resistance to evictions came to a head at Drummin, Woodford, County Galway, with the so-called 'Siege of Sanders Fort'. A number of men barricaded themselves into the house of Thomas Sanders, who was to be evicted. Although they were eventually overcome, their resistance was widely publicised and captured the imagination of many nationalists both at home and abroad.[4]

And so it was into these turbulent times that Éamonn Ceannt and many other men and women who took part in the 1916 Easter Rebellion were born. By the turn of the nineteenth century, the old Fenians and separatists were passing on their ideals to a new generation of young Irish people. The foundation of nationalist organisations such as the Gaelic League and Sinn Féin helped to instil a renewed pride in Irish history and culture and provided a stage for the many young people who were anxious to display an Irish identity. Éamonn Ceannt was among the many young people who became involved with these organisations, and other similar movements, which were designed to encourage a nationalist future for Ireland.[5]

2

From Birth to Manhood

For Éamonn Ceannt life began on 21 September 1881 in the pleasant little village of Ballymoe, overlooking the River Suck in County Galway. Ceannt's birth certificate registered him as Edward Thomas Kent. Ironically he was born in the barracks of the RIC, where his father, James Kent, was a constable. Some sources indicate that James Kent was born near Ballyporeen, County Tipperary, in 1841. However, prior to his death in 1912, his son Michael, recording family information, noted that his father once stated that he was born on 4 July 1839, just before the 'Night of the Big Wind' (6 July) at Rehill in the parish of Clogheen, near Mitchelstown, County Cork. James had three brothers, Bill, Phillip and Michael, and two sisters, Mary and Margaret. Their parents were from Rehill. James's mother was Ellen Cleary and, according to family tradition, she was descended from one of the families of the Four Masters. James's father died in 1895 at the age of ninety-three and was buried in an old family plot in a graveyard near Shanrahan on the road to Ballyporeen.

Michael recalled that at the time there was already an old headstone over the grave inscribed with the name William Kent, an ancestor. The Kents were a Roman Catholic family living in the rural setting of a farming community.

On 15 January 1862, James joined the RIC. Following his training, on 13 May he was appointed to service in Cork. Presumably it was while serving in Cork that he met his wife, Joanne Galway. Her family was originally from Waterford, but moved to Cork where Joanne was born. They were married on 5 July 1870. On 10 October 1873, James was transferred to Ballymoe, County Galway. According to family records the last four of their seven children were born at Ballymoe. In order of birth the children were: William, Michael, Richard, Nell, John, Éamonn and James. William later followed a military career and eventually became a colour sergeant major with the Royal Dublin Fusiliers. Michael became a chief clerk with the Dublin City engineering department. He married Julia Anne Gibney and they had four children: Joan, Alice, Nora and Éamonn. It is thanks to Nora's daughters, Mary and the late Joan Gallagher, that so much information has come to light regarding Éamonn Ceannt. Richard also married and had three children: Kathleen, Maureen and Joan. Nell, the only sister, married a man named Jack Casey. John worked for the Dublin Shipyard Company at North Wall. Very little is recorded about James.[1]

On 21 October 1883, James Kent was promoted to head constable at Ballymoe and exactly two months later he was transferred to Ardee, County Louth. While living in Ardee, Éamonn attended the De La Salle national school. All the family were devout Catholics and he became an altar-boy; his religious teaching as a child stayed with him for the remainder of his life. He was an extremely shy child and became nervous in the company of strangers, unlike his brothers who were described as 'wild and sturdy'. He had a great ability to absorb knowledge and because of this his brothers gave him the nickname 'Wiseacre'. From an early age he showed remarkable powers of observation and had an excellent memory. He enjoyed rambling across the bogs, fishing and birdwatching, and could mimic the calls of the various birds with great accuracy. He also liked to attend the occasional slide show in the town and, of course, go to any visiting circus.

Éamonn spent five years at De La Salle before the family moved to Drogheda, where he attended the Christian Brothers School in Sunday's Gate.[2]

On 15 April 1892, James Kent retired from the RIC and the family moved to Dublin. They first lived at Bayview Avenue, Fairview, but shortly afterwards moved to 232 Clonliffe Road, Drumcondra. Éamonn was eleven when he began attending the North Richmond Street Christian Brothers School. It was one of a number of schools opened by Edmund Rice, the founder of the Christian Brothers, and Daniel O'Connell laid the foundation stone in 1828. Because of O'Connell's involvement in the foundation of these schools they became widely known as O'Connell

Schools. In 1895 Éamonn's mother died; he was deeply affected but displayed remarkable composure and remained silent throughout the mourning period.

Although most sources indicate that he was a diligent worker, overall he seems to have been an average student and a 'bit of a character'. Sport played a role in his youth, particularly rugby until it was banned from the school by one of the teachers. An earlier ban had stopped them from playing the game in school grounds, but now there was a full prohibition on the sport even outside the school. Nevertheless, this did not deter Éamonn and his friends as they carried on playing regardless of the ban. They even formed a team called Branavilla Rovers; how well the team played is not known. His other sports included hurling, and he played many games in the Phoenix Park.[3]

He was obviously being tutored in Irish history, because on 11 October 1896 he made the following brief entry in his school diary: 'Anniversary of a man named Parnell's demise. Made my debut as an orator today, before an audience of two in the drawing school.' On 30 October 1896, he records: 'Mr Maunsell "instruction" week. He waxed enthusiastic about love of country.' Another entry mentions a composition in favour of nationalism entitled: 'A good cause makes a stout heart.' On 5 April 1897, he signed his name in Irish for the first time in his school diary.

In 1898, along with many of his school companions, he took part in the centenary celebrations commemorating the 1798 rebellion. It was a time of a tremendous revival in the national spirit and Éamonn became intensely inflamed with the idea of nationalism. This type of reaction to his beliefs was a typical feature of his character. It is interesting to note, however, that while at school he did not study Irish, which at the time was an optional subject. He did study French and German and, in order to improve his grasp of them, made a habit of spending afternoons at the Dublin port talking to sailors from various continental countries.

Although his diaries do not indicate an academic career, his interest in education obviously changed after this time. He achieved excellent results in his final exams in 1898, taking honours papers in French, German, Algebra, Arithmetic, Euclid and Precis Writing and pass papers in Latin, English, Plane Trigonometry and Shorthand, and he achieved the highest results in all papers.

At the school's prize-giving day banquet in 1898 he was one of the speakers. It was customary for distinguished students to be asked to give a speech at the school awards and for their families to attend. Because of his shyness as a boy, Éamonn's family didn't have great hopes for his performance. They took their seats in the hall feeling that he would forfeit the awards rather than face the audience. But to their utter amazement Éamonn stepped forward on the platform and spoke eloquently of the school's achievements. This was his first time to speak before an audience and his father exclaimed: 'My boy Éamonn will do something great yet.'

On leaving school he applied for a job as a reporter

with the *Irish Independent*, but on hearing of the working hours required, he decided against it. He also had the opportunity to work with the civil service, but felt that he would be working for the British and so turned down the position. He decided instead to sit an examination for a post within Dublin Corporation and in the meantime acted as an assistant teacher at the North Richmond Street school. The results of the corporation exam secured him a position with the clerical staff of the City Treasurer and Estates and Finances Office. His salary on appointment was £70 per annum, with an annual increment of £5.

In 1899 hostilities broke out between the British and the Dutch farmers – more commonly known as 'Boers' – of the Orange Free State and the South African Republic. The trouble had begun in 1886, when the Uitlanders, who were mainly British subjects, rushed to the Witwatersrand gold fields. The Boers denied them any political right or power. By the close of the nineteenth century the situation had developed into the Boer War and, in the early stages, the Boers won some victories. However, the British poured in reinforcements, among them Éamonn's brother, William. By Christmas 1899, the war was raging furiously and because of the many Irishmen caught up in the conflict, one would imagine that there would have been considerable anti-Boer feeling in Ireland. However, the reality was very different, at least in the west of Ireland. At a meeting of the Galway Guardians on 20 December 1899, a resolution was passed congratulating the Boers on their victories and wishing them ultimate success: a move which gives some idea of the prevalent anti-British feelings. Éamonn asked his sister, Nell, to make a Boer flag, which he then mounted on a tree at the end of the garden. It remained there for a number of days until the flag was brought to the attention of his father, who had it removed immediately. This was Éamonn's first demonstration of defiance against England and it seems he was disappointed when the Boers were eventually defeated and forced to surrender in May 1902.[4]

3

Contribution to the Gaelic Revival

In 1899, Ceannt joined the central branch of the Gaelic League, which at that time was holding its meetings at 24 Upper Sackville (now O'Connell) Street, Dublin, and it was here that he first met Patrick Pearse and Eoin MacNeill. The purpose of the Gaelic League was to revive not just the Irish language, but also Irish music, dancing, poetry, literature and history, to educate people in Irish culture and to give them a new sense of pride in their heritage. One of the main practical achievements of the Gaelic League was the introduction of Irish as a subject in primary schools. The league spread quickly throughout Ireland, eventually establishing about 600 branches. Joining the league was a very important step in Ceannt's life as it was through this organisation that he developed a deeper devotion to Irish nationalism and made many friends who shared the same ideologies. He became immersed in the organisation and was soon recognised as one of the most earnest workers of its central branch. Because of his commitment, he was eventually elected as a member of its governing body.[1]

While his brothers and friends went to dances and other events, Ceannt would remain at home studying Irish. He was a keen reader and always carried a book in his pocket to read while on tram journeys. He spent a lot of time in the National Library of Ireland and most of his summer holidays, Easter and other long weekends in the west of Ireland. Apart from perfecting his Irish, he continued to add to the store of Irish music, stories and traditions already collected for his portfolio. Such was his knowledge and fluency that he became one of the Gaelic League's pioneering Irish teachers. By 1905 he was teaching Irish language classes in branch offices of the league. According to his family Ceannt eventually spoke Irish 'beautifully – richly, quietly, with humour'. As early as 1902 he was generally recognised as one of the best Irish teachers in Dublin – quite an achievement when one considers that he began to study the language seriously only in 1898. It seems his father may have given him some tutoring also.[2]

During this period he was also influencing the revival of Irish music and, in particular, the Irish war and uileann pipes. So strong was his love of Irish culture that he decided to embrace traditional music and he chose the pipes as his main instrument (he could also play the flute, tin-whistle and violin). At one point Ceannt and some family members even formed the 'Kent Brother Band'. In February 1900, Ceannt, along with Edward Martyn of Tulira, County

Galway, helped with the foundation of Cumann na bPíobairí (The Pipers' Club) in Dublin. He obviously used his influence with the Gaelic League to secure a venue for Cumann na bPíobairí, as the minutes of the meeting record the league's Sackville Street address.[3]

Shortly after the foundation of The Pipers' Club, Ceannt bought a printing press on which he printed a journal, *An Píobaire*, to help promote the club; the first edition was published on 5 July 1901. *An Píobaire* covered all references to pipes from earliest times and included articles in Irish. It was also intended to transcribe related articles from *The Dublin Penny Journal*.

The first Annual General Meeting of Cumann na bPíobairí was held on 1 February 1901. In the election of officers, Ceannt successfully proposed Dr J. St Clair Boyd for the position of president. Ceannt was elected honorary secretary. At this meeting the rules were revised, including the name of the club to which they added the words 'Baile Átha Cliath'. The second rule of the club stated, 'That Irish shall, as far as possible, be the official language of the club' – possibly another reason for Ceannt's quick command of the language. Cumann na bPíobairí also taught its members to play the fiddle and provided lessons in Irish dancing and singing. The committee immediately set about promoting the club nationally and it was decided to invite – at the club's expense – a number of pipers from around the country to attend the Leinster feis. Among those invited were two Galway pipers, Martin Reilly of Eyre Street and

Pat McDonagh of Spanish Parade. Martin Reilly became a personal friend of Ceannt and always stayed with him when visiting Dublin.

In 1901 Ceannt left his home in Clonliffe Road and moved to 22 Fairview Avenue, Clontarf. By 1902 Cumann na bPíobairí was holding its meetings every Friday at 7.30 p.m. in 41 Rutland Square. In the same year he was instrumental in having pipers from other countries visit Ireland, as can be seen from the following letter:

> Cumann na bPíobairí Pipers' Club
> 41 Rutland Square, Dublin
> Rev. Dear Sir,
> I have much pleasure in acknowledging receipt of both your letters informing Cumann na bPíobairí that you were coming to Ireland and had been deputed to call on us bearing greetings and good wishes from our brother pipers in Chicago. Accept our hearty thanks and be assured that in whatever capacity you come, the Gaels of Ireland will extend to you a Céad Míle Fáilte. My committee are desirous of organising a little reception in your honour and if you give us a week's notice we shall do so. If you intend coming on here within a week after landing, we shall be glad to get notices of your coming so that you may be given an opportunity of hearing us at our best. The club meets on Fridays at the above address.
>
> Hoping to receive a reply advising us of your arrival and intention to visit Dublin, and trusting you have had a pleasant passage.
> Do Com. Píobaire
> Éamonn Ceannt
> Edw. T. Kent. Hon. Sec.[4]

Ceannt was also mainly responsible for the inclusion of pipe music in competitions on Feis Cheoil programmes by using his influence with various organisers with whom he was acquainted. As a result, he was invited by many organising committees to act as adjudicator in events held around the country. One feis that he attended was held in Killeeneen, County Galway and, having heard a local tale there about Anthony Raftery, he is reputed to have written the poem below. It seems that in 1900, thanks to Lady Gregory, a cross had been erected over the grave of the great Gaelic poet, Raftery, who had been buried in a paupers' grave in Killeeneen graveyard; a feis was also organised to celebrate the event. An old man named Terence Furey had identified the grave for Lady Gregory. He stated that Raftery had been buried at night because the coffin had been late arriving from the town of Gort and that because Raftery was a pauper his body had been taken to the paupers' plot:

> What means the crowd of people, what means the beat of
>   drum?
> Why go they to the churchyard, from whereforth have they
>   come?
> Why gather here the rich and poor from east, west, south
>   and north?
> There's someone speaking to the throng and ringing cheers
>   go forth.
> I put these different questions to an old and feeble man
> Whose hair was white as drifted snow, whose face was thin
>   and wan

And though old age had done its work, yet still his merry eye
Lit up with kind and pleasant smile and then he made reply.
'Tis now three score and five long years, since I was but a boy
There passed away our Gaelic bard to the land of peace and joy,
His soul's with God, his body's here in Killeeneen old
    churchyard,
And sure every Irish man has heard of Raftery the bard.
'Twas he could tell the story, 'twas he could sing the song
In our own old native language too for he hated the Saxon
    tongue,
And on a Sunday evening when the boys and girls would come
And listen there with willing air to Raftery's latest poem
Or dance an Irish jig or reel while Raftery would play
Upon his good old fiddle his comrade night and day
We had no foreign dances then, sure that was in the time
When Raftery was amongst us and I was in my prime.
The grand old Irish speeches with cheers the people hail,
In remembrance of Raftery, the poet, saint, and Gael.
So now we have come to erect a cross above his grave today
So then you've got the reason why the crowds have come
    this way.
And here in auld Killeeneen where the wintry winds do rave
A cross now stands – an Irish cross – o'er his long lost grave.
And all around are headstones like sentinels and guards
To protect the bones of Raftery, the last of Ireland's bards.

On St Patrick's Day 1902, the Gaelic League organised a 'Language Procession' in Dublin. It was Ceannt's idea and he took part in the march, sounding the war pipes to signal the beginning of the rally. The procession was a huge success; the Gaelic League had ventured out of the 'catacombs' into the streets of the capital to the admiration of the people who lined the route. Only one noticeable disruption occurred when about 700 members announced that they had to leave the parade to turn up for work in Dublin's licensed premises. The following year the Gaelic League appealed to the pub owners to remain closed for St Patrick's Day, but the request fell on deaf ears. Most of the organisers, among them Ceannt, believed that the idea of 'drowning the shamrock' was shocking. Their slogan was: 'Do not drown the shamrock; wear it unstilled; wear it proudly.' A plan was put in place for the following year and at the beginning of 1903 a countrywide campaign began to ensure that all pubs remained closed on St Patrick's Day, and to have the authorities declare it a national holiday. In the end all their efforts were in vain, but the 'Language Procession' of 1903 turned out to be a phenomenal success, with many additional schools and bands taking part, and larger crowds than the previous year lining the route.[5]

Ceannt's great devotion to the pipes continued throughout his life and for years he tried, with remarkable success, to restore the popularity of Irish pipe music. An old friend, Martin Daly, recorded his feeling upon hearing Ceannt's music:

> … they stir the blood with the strangest exhilarations, the subtlest intimations: I hear the voice of Ireland in the pipes; in the distance the thin, coiling cry of the pipes turns me cold with the sense of the far off sad romance of our country; close at hand whether they moan or exult or simply croon their

long soft memories they tell me – in a beautiful phrase, once English but Irish now for a very sufficient reason – they tell me of 'old unhappy far-off things and of battles long ago'.[6]

4

Falling in Love

Frances Mary O'Brennan was born in Dublin on 23 September 1880. Áine, as she became known, was the youngest of four daughters, the others being Mary, Lily and Kathleen (the latter a journalist and playwright), born to Frank and Elizabeth O'Brennan *née* Butler. Áine never knew her father as he died about four months before she was born. Frank O'Brennan was originally from Tipperary and, as a young man, had been involved in the Fenian movement. It was in connection with this that he had arrived in Dublin, supposedly disguised as a pedlar. He was also an auctioneer and had spent a number of years in America before being married. He died after a short illness leaving his young wife Elizabeth, who was still only in her twenties, with four children to care for and educate. There is very little known of Áine's family background, except that she was a great-grand-niece of the Most Reverend Dr Tobias Kirby, Archbishop of Ephesus and Rector of the Irish College in Rome for over fifty years. Dr Kirby was born in January 1804 in Tallow, County Waterford, and according to family tradition his father had been a member of the Society of United Irishmen. On the night Dr Kirby was born, his father is reputed to have been still in hiding after Robert Emmet's rising of 1803. Having moved to Rome, Dr Kirby became a close friend of Pope Leo XIII and, following Kirby's death, the pope wrote an elegy which is inscribed on the Kirby statue in the memorial hall of the Vatican. Éamonn Ceannt later went to view this monument while on a visit to Rome in 1908.[1]

Áine was educated at the Dominican College, Eccles Street, Dublin. Even as a child she had a strong interest in Irish culture and upon leaving school joined the Gaelic League central branch. It was on the league's annual excursion to Galway in 1901 that Áine first met Ceannt. She later recorded her train journey to Galway in glorious summer weather and said that it was Ceannt's 'wonderful whistling, sweet as a bird on a bush', that first drew her attention to him. She stated that he was then in his nineteenth year, was 'tall, handsome and slight' and at first appeared older than his actual age. She was also attracted by his sense of humour and the manner in which his eyes sparkled as he looked at her throughout the journey. Once the train crossed the River Shannon at Athlone, Ceannt called for 'three cheers' for the people of Connacht. He also lost no opportunity to shout greetings in Irish to people standing on the station platforms as the train made its way westward. Although he had left Galway at a young age, Ceannt always took great pride in letting people know he was a Galwegian.[2]

Sketch of Áine by her husband,
Éamonn Ceannt, in 1907
(*courtesy of the Allen Library*).

Upon reaching Galway the two had dinner, after which they set off on a tour of the city. They then spent most of the journey home together. According to one source it was Áine's 'gentleness and sweetness' which appealed to his chivalry. They continued to see each other, sometimes through their involvement with the league. Following this outing, Áine joined Cumann na bPíobairí and shortly afterwards was appointed treasurer while Ceannt was still secretary. They certainly shared a common passion for Irish culture and a keen relationship soon blossomed into love.[3]

Ceannt developed an excellent relationship with the O'Brennan family and was particularly fond of Áine's mother, Elizabeth. One of Áine's sisters, Lily, was very fond of Ceannt, as is apparent from her later writings. At the time she recorded a short descriptive image of Ceannt, stating that he was a quiet, unassuming man, who was rather reserved in the presence of strangers, but that he possessed an 'active sense of humour'. She remembered too that his large hazel eyes were serious, but perhaps somewhat dreamy and that he always kept his moustache trimmed. He was a very disciplined man who never drank or smoked, and the virtues he praised most in life were truth and charity.[4]

One female acquaintance of Ceannt's stated that at that time Ceannt did not fully agree with women in politics, and that she once had an argument with him regarding the issue. However, she went on to say that although he was a bit on the serious side, he was at times full of 'dash and fire'. Martin Daly stated that there were few human beings towards whom he felt such warmth and even fewer still that he held in the same 'hoping admiration'. He recorded that Ceannt was tall, almost six foot, handsome, always coolly self-possessed and faced the world with a commanding presence.[5]

At Christmas 1903, Ceannt proposed to Áine and their marriage took place on 7 June 1905 in St James's Church in Dublin. A family friend, Fr Anderson, returned from France to perform the ceremony. The ceremony was conducted in Irish, and the couple insisted on using French coins, rather than the English ones which carried the emblem of the British crown. They received a papal blessing from Pope Pius X to mark the occasion. It is not known if Ceannt's brothers, James and William, attended the wedding as James died of tuberculosis sometime in 1905 and William was serving with the Royal Dublin Fusiliers in Malta at the time. Following the wedding the young couple lived in rented accommodation at 44 Reuben Avenue, South Circular Road. It was while living at this address that their only child, Rónán, was born a year later on 18 June 1906.[6]

Ceannt continued to visit Galway whenever he had time. On occasion in Dublin he would produce sods of turf which he would set alight, impale on a poker and walk with them throughout the house, saying that the smell would remind him of Galway. Áine later stated that he spent all of his holidays in the west of Ireland and that 'every piper knew him'. A lot of his time was spent in Spiddal where he played the pipes at ceilidhes held in houses around the village, entertaining local teenagers and students from the Irish college. One of his friends, whom he often stayed with in Spiddal, was Michael Thornton, a man with whom he remained in contact until the rebellion.

At the 1906 Oireachtas Ceannt's musical talent for the pipes won him the gold medal. His reputation as a piper was being nationally acclaimed and in September 1908 he travelled to Rome with a group of Irish athletes who were members of the Catholic Young Men's Society. The society had felt that it was necessary to indicate as strongly as possible that Ireland was represented as a separate nation and found a very willing participant in Ceannt when they approached him to act as the official Irish piper. Ceannt dressed in an ancient style Irish green and red costume specially produced for the event. The occasion of the pilgrimage was to celebrate the jubilee of Pope Pius X. The International Federation of Catholic Young Men's Societies organised the international athletic competitions to be held in the Vatican gardens that year. All countries throughout Europe were represented, with the exception of England. The Irish group left the North Wall, Dublin, to tremendous cheering and the strains of Ceannt playing 'God Bless the Pope'. According to reliable sources, Ceannt played throughout the journey and was the 'life and soul' of the pilgrimage.[7]

One of the highlights for the Irish group was an audience with the pope. Care was taken prior to the event to inform the holy father that he would hear an instrument that had not been heard in Rome for hundreds of years, some said not since the glory days of the earls of Ulster. Upon entering the pontiff's chamber, the Irish group formed themselves into three sides of a square, the fourth side being occupied by the papal throne. The pope then delivered an address, after which the gathering began to sing 'Song for the Pope'. Just as the last note of the song was dying away, the sound of a piper playing the opening bars of 'O'Donnell Abú' wafted through the chamber as Ceannt made his appearance, having slipped out during the singing to change into his costume and collect the pipes. He marched directly to the steps of the throne and continued playing. When he had finished, the pope asked him to come forward so he could examine the pipes, after which he requested another performance. Ceannt complied by playing 'The Wearing of the Green'. After the performance the pope bestowed an apostolic blessing on Ceannt. Among the other tunes Ceannt played was 'I Won't be a Nun'.

While in Rome, Ceannt took the opportunity to visit the Kirby monument and recorded details of the memorial, which he then sent to Áine. He also sent a greeting card to a Dublin alderman, Tom Kelly, who would later play an unsuspecting role in the lead-up to the rebellion. Before returning, Ceannt viewed the Black Sea and then visited China.[8]

5

Path to Rebellion

In 1907 Ceannt joined the Dublin central branch of Sinn Féin. Shortly afterwards he was elected to the committee of that branch and was eventually elected onto the national council. Arthur Griffith had founded the Sinn Féin movement in 1905. Similar to Ceannt, Griffith had a great love for the Irish language and once declared that: 'No country could give up its language and retain its soul.' Griffith was a huge force in the spreading of Irish nationalism and inspired a generation of young Irishmen, among them Éamonn Ceannt.[1]

During the period from 1906 to 1912, Ceannt was involved in a number of activities. He was engaged in a small gardening business and was contemplating putting his artistic endeavours to use in setting up an advertising agency. Day to day working life continued as normal for him in Dublin Corporation. The corporation records show that he was soon entrusted with the duties of a wages clerk and eventually ended up as a junior official in the finance department, earning up to £200 per annum by 1915.

Ceannt was extremely punctual and very popular with his colleagues and it seems that his sincerity, determination and thoroughness were the hallmarks of his success in negotiations. He was voted in as an executive on the Dublin Municipal Officers' Association, a movement initiated to look after the interests of office clerks. The following year he was voted chairman of the organisation. As a staunch believer in workers' rights, he threw himself with great diligence into the work of the organisation. He proved himself an excellent chairman and his term was characterised by a number of successful schemes introduced to improve his colleagues' positions. His speeches at some of the organisation's social functions have been described as 'masterpieces'. Ceannt was obviously in some demand at this time as a speaker because, according to Áine, he was asked to give a lecture on constitutional agitation to the Irish Socialist Party in the Antient Concert Rooms, Dublin, in 1910 and also spoke about the Irish pipes and pipers at a series of lectures held in the National Museum of Ireland.[2]

In 1911, King George V planned a visit to Ireland in July. As preparations got underway in Dublin for the royal visit, nationalists were planning a very different reception for the king. A body called the United National Societies Committee was formed and met at the Sinn Féin headquarters in Harcourt Street. The committee consisted of Éamonn Ceannt, his friend and work colleague, Seán Fitzgibbon, Michael Joseph O'Rahilly, historically known as The O'Rahilly, and three other members who would later sign the Proclamation: Seán Mac Diarmada, Thomas MacDonagh and Patrick Pearse. The principal objective of the new committee was to organise public opinion against the royal visit and to prevent Dublin Corporation from presenting a 'loyal address'. The committee was not very successful, however, as the streets of Dublin were completely decorated with flags and banners welcoming the king. Nevertheless, Ceannt's spirit was not dampened. Through his contacts within Dublin Corporation and with the help of his colleague, Seán Fitzgibbon, he managed to have a banner erected across the road just outside Trinity College. The following morning Dubliners were astonished to see the banner draped across Grafton Street announcing: 'Thou art not conquered yet, dear Land.' As soon as the authorities were informed, the police removed the banner.

At this point there was no hope of stopping the royal celebrations and because of this a large number of nationalists decided to leave Dublin. They organised a pilgrimage to Wolfe Tone's grave in Bodenstown. On the return journey the train was deliberately held up for half an hour between Inchicore and Kingsbridge (Heuston) station, so that the nationalists would not clash with those taking part in the celebrations. During the royal visit there was a protest meeting held at Foster Place but there was only one arrest.

The extreme nationalists availed of every opportunity to show their disloyalty and Ceannt was now ranking among this group. When the viceroy, Lord Aberdeen, was invited to a concert held by the Catholic Boys' Brigade in the Rotunda, Ceannt, Seán Fitzgibbon and some others made their way to the concert hall with the avowed intention of protesting against the presence of the royal representative. They were, of course, ejected and detained outside by police until Lord Aberdeen had left the premises.[3]

At that time the burning question for many nationalists was home rule and whether the British government would implement it, thus allowing Irishmen to govern Ireland. Isaac Butt had founded the Home Rule League in 1870 and the issue had dominated Irish affairs since Charles Stewart Parnell took over the leadership of the Irish Parliamentary Party following Butt's death in 1879.[4]

Between 1910 and 1911 two events occurred which were to change the pattern of Anglo-Irish politics. The first was the general election of 1910 which produced a hung parliament for the liberal prime minister, H. H. Asquith. The liberals could stay in power only with the support of the Irish Nationalist Party, and the price for its cooperation was home rule. The second event was the Parliament Act of 1911, which deprived the House of Lords of their ancient power to obstruct legislation. This meant that home rule could be delayed for only two years because after that time it automatically became the law of the land. So when Asquith introduced the third Irish home rule bill in 1912, it seemed that Ireland was only two years away from a certain degree of independence.

However, to many people home rule was still only a dream and it caused frustration among the nationalists. On 31 March 1912, a home rule rally was held in Dublin. The speakers included Joseph Devlin, MP, Eoin MacNeill, John Redmond (leader of the Irish Nationalist Party) and Patrick Pearse. Pearse spoke in Irish and was clearly more determined than any of the others on the home rule issue. He stated that if they were deceived, he would advise the Irish people against consultation with the British, declaring they would 'answer them with violence and the edge of a sword. Let the English understand that if we are again betrayed there shall be red war throughout Ireland.' It seems that Éamonn Ceannt remained silent on this issue. Áine believed he did so because he did not want to draw attention to the fact that at that stage he had strong feelings on the matter of an independent Ireland. Sinn Féin boycotted the rally, believing among other things that the home rule bill would be rejected. Although Ceannt's view on home rule may have differed to Pearse's, they were both very committed to independence. So much so that when on 16 March 1912 Pearse launched his own newspaper, *An Barr Buadh* (*The Trumpet of Victory*), he did so with the support of Ceannt and some others. Men who shared Pearse's political principles produced this newspaper in Irish. Although the paper ran for only eleven issues, Ceannt was its most prolific and significant contributor.

The day after the newspaper's launch Ceannt's father died. It is not known how his father's death affected

Ceannt, but he subsequently became more deeply involved with the nationalist movement; on 12 December 1912 he recorded in his diary: '*Is iongantach an lá é seo, is iongantach an lá domsa freisin é*' (This is a wonderful day, it's a wonderful day for me also). Áine believed that it was on this date that Ceannt joined the IRB, the secret oath-bound Irish revolutionary group. Ceannt was sworn into the organisation by Seán Mac Diarmada and never faltered when declaring the IRB oath:

> In the presence of God I Éamonn Ceannt do solemnly swear that I will do my utmost to establish the national independence of Ireland, and that I will bear true allegiance to the Supreme Council of the Irish Republican Brotherhood and Government of the Irish Republic and implicitly obey the Constitution of the Irish Republican Brotherhood and all my superior officers and that I will preserve inviolable the secrets of the organisation.

James Stephens had launched the IRB in Dublin on St Patrick's Day 1858. The movement was pledged to achieve Irish independence and to do so by physical force if necessary. Since its foundation it had been behind every Irish organisation with separatist ideals and survived for many years with financial support from the Fenian movement in America.

The IRB took every opportunity to train their personnel in the use of firearms and early in 1913 the Banda Rifle Club was formed. A short time later a meeting of the

Sinn Féin national council was held. Éamonn Ceannt put forward a proposal that all its members should be trained in the use of firearms, stating, 'It is the duty of every Irishman to possess a knowledge of arms.' He believed that the time had come for rebellion and that nationalists should avail of any military training. Arthur Griffith was not present at this meeting and was very indignant when he heard of Ceannt's proposal. Later, when speaking to The O'Rahilly, he said that he wanted no 'tinpike soldiers' who were incapable of serious conflict. The O'Rahilly assured Griffith that he need not worry about Ceannt and that he evidently didn't know him very well. He went on to say that any assignment Ceannt undertook he completed, and that he would do the same on this issue, adding that Ceannt was already being instructed in the use of firearms. In fact, Ceannt had set up a firing range at his home in Bloomsfield where he lived for a short time. It seems that after this conversation Griffith was satisfied.[5]

Meanwhile the path to home rule was proving extremely difficult, with a bitter and frenzied response from the Tories to the likelihood of home rule. Their answer was to enlist the services of Ulster Unionist, Sir Edward Carson, in opposition to the bill. Carson persuaded 80,000 Belfast unionists to sign a document against home rule and many of them did so in their own blood. The unionists in Ulster announced that they would fight the United Kingdom in order to remain part of it. This led to the foundation of the Ulster Volunteer Force on 31 January 1913. As the reality of the limited independence of home rule came closer, opposition became more serious, with Carson being supported by some of the military. In March 1914 fifty-eight senior British officers at the Curragh in County Kildare said that they would refuse to enforce home rule in Ulster. This incident is often referred to as the 'Curragh Mutiny'.[6]

Ceannt continued to visit Galway and the Aran Islands in the years leading up to 1916. On occasions he was accompanied by Pearse and another revolutionary, Joseph Plunkett, while making contact with republicans in Galway, as his address book can testify. The address book contains the names and addresses of leading Galway rebels at the time and many other contacts throughout Ireland. While in Aran they stayed at St Rónán's in Kilronan. The late Bridget Dirrane, author of *A Woman of Aran*, recorded in her book that Ceannt and the others were regular visitors and that she often served them tea at the Concannon home. At the time Bridget was told not to divulge any information she might overhear while serving at the table. A few years later, Bridget also became involved in the republican movement by joining Cumann na mBan.[7]

6

Foundation of the Irish Volunteers

On 10 November 1913, The O'Rahilly invited Ceannt to attend a meeting which was to be held in Wynn's Hotel, Dublin the following day. The purpose of the meeting was to decide on the formation of the Irish Volunteer Force, which was welcomed by all who attended. It was late that night when Ceannt returned home and upon arrival he found the fire brigade trying to control a huge fire in the neighbouring yard. Ceannt believed that the fire had been set maliciously and had been intended for his home. However, this did not deter him and, once the decision was taken to form the Irish Volunteers, Ceannt and the others lost no time in getting the movement off the ground with a public meeting being arranged for 25 November at the Rotunda Rink, Dublin.

The venue could cater for 4,000 people, but about 7,000 attended and a number of speakers, including Pearse and MacNeill, addressed the large gathering. By this time

Pearse was becoming a very important figure on the Irish political scene. Overall the meeting was a huge success, with 3,000 recruits signing up immediately for the new Volunteer force. According to Áine, it was agreed prior to the meeting that Ceannt and a number of other extreme nationalists would not speak at the meeting to avoid attracting any attention, as the British authorities were keeping a careful eye on the situation. Ceannt went on ahead to the meeting, followed a little later by Áine and her sister Lily. Eoin MacNeill was elected chief-of-staff of the Irish Volunteers and within ten months its ranks had swollen to 180,000. It was 1 December 1913 before Ceannt officially enrolled in the Volunteers.

Although the Fianna Éireann (nationalist youth movement) already existed, the immediate success of the Irish Volunteers prompted Pearse to suggest the formation of a new Irish youth movement, Buachaillí na hÉireann. A small committee was set up to launch this organisation and Áine Ceannt became involved, as did Tom Clarke and Kerry Reddin. A large meeting was held in the national school in Sheriff Street and Pearse addressed the gathering. Another revolutionary who attended the meeting was Liam Mellows who was on the executive of Fianna Éireann at the time. Mellows promised Áine that he would help in setting up the new movement. However, others who attended the meeting were not in favour of another youth movement and the idea of Buachaillí na hÉireann was abandoned.

The IRB was a secret organisation with strong separatist ideals, and because of this it could not acquire mass support without attracting the attention of the British authorities. The Irish Volunteers provided the ideal cover for the IRB as it now had an open military force which could be used to achieve its aims. Eoin MacNeill was not aware of the influence that the IRB held within the movement and three key members of the IRB, Pearse, Ceannt and Seán Mac Diarmada, were elected to the Volunteer committee. Their plan was to infiltrate and eventually take over the organisation so that when the time was right it could be used as their own revolutionary army.[1]

Labour leaders James Larkin and James Connolly founded another revolutionary army, the Irish Citizen Army, on 19 November 1913. There was a huge amount of social unrest in Dublin during this period, much of it due to a bitter strike which led to the Dublin 'lock-out'. Labour disputes at the time had escalated into a general strike and James Larkin urged members of his union to stop handling goods belonging to William Murphy, the most formidable employer in Dublin. Murphy reacted by getting an agreement from other employers to 'lock out' Larkin's union members. The Irish Citizen Army was established as a workers' defence corps and its initial purpose was to enable workers to defend themselves in clashes with the police. Éamonn Ceannt supported Larkin's labour movement and this situation possibly helped to swell the ranks of the newly formed Irish Volunteers.

By Christmas 1913 Ceannt was contributing to the Volunteer gazette. He was taking his role in the new movement very seriously and displayed strong feelings towards military training. Through his writings he was reaching and influencing a much wider audience:

> Stoop your back to the burden. Keep your eye clear, and your nerves steady. Be skilled in the arts of war, and there will be no war. Live plainly, so that you may be strong and hardy. Be not given to vain boasting. Do not tarry long in taverns nor take counsel with those who would betray you. Keep your own counsel. Be simple, be efficient, be noble, and the world of Ireland is yours.[2]

In February 1914 the Volunteer provisional constitution was issued and its objectives included: 'To secure and maintain the rights and liberties common to all the people of Ireland; to train, discipline, arm and equip a body of Irish Volunteers for the above purpose; to unite for this purpose Irishmen of every creed and every party and class.' Shortly afterwards, subcommittees were formed on which a disproportionate number of IRB members were allowed to sit. The actual size of the movement became a concern for the IRB as its numbers within the Volunteers countrywide were not sufficient to influence and control the movement. For instance, Éamonn Ceannt stood alone among the six members of Dublin city and county subcommittees.

Volunteers were also being recruited and trained abroad, and they included Michael Collins and the Galway writer,

Pádraic Ó Conaire. Both men took part in manoeuvres together while living in London.[3]

John Redmond, the leader of the Irish Nationalist Party, was at first against the formation of the Irish Volunteers and tried to discourage people from joining the movement. However, the Ancient Order of Hibernians fully supported the new movement, and even asked its members to join the Volunteers. Redmond, realising just how strong the new movement was becoming, requested that some of his nominees be placed on the executive committee. His request was at first refused, but at a meeting of the provisional committee on 16 June 1914, twenty-five of Redmond's representatives were accepted. Among those who opposed Redmond's demands were Ceannt, Pearse and Mellows. Nevertheless, in the interest of unity, the IRB men reluctantly accepted the committee's decision to allow Redmond's nominees to join the committee. With his own followers now on the inside, Redmond gained much control within the movement.[4]

In May 1914 Cumann na mBan had been formed as part of the Irish Volunteers and, following its amalgamation with Inghinidhe na hÉireann, it became the main women's organisation throughout Ireland. Áine attended the first meeting and joined the movement, soon being appointed to its central branch. Jenny Wyse Power, Kathleen Clarke and Áine's sister, Lily, also joined the movement.[5]

7

Gun-Running

The tense situation in Ulster led to the illegal importation of arms at Larne, County Antrim, in April 1914, with the Ulster Volunteer Force landing a consignment of arms consisting of 20,000 rifles and almost three million rounds of ammunition. The Irish Volunteers were well aware of the situation developing in Ulster and were also preparing to arm themselves. On 26 July 1914 the Irish Volunteers landed a shipment of over 900 Mauser rifles and 26,000 rounds of ammunition at Howth, County Dublin. The yacht *Asgard*, owned by an English-born sympathiser, Erskine Childers, was used for the transportation of the arms. Childers' son, also called Erskine, later became president of Ireland. Ceannt was in command of one of the sections responsible for the distribution of the arms. As the Volunteers returned to Dublin the military intercepted them. During the confrontation Ceannt drew his pistol and fired on the British soldiers. Most sources maintain that a catastrophe was avoided because the soldiers thought that the shots had come from the onlooking crowd.

Later that day troops of the King's Own Scottish Borderers opened fire on a crowd that had gathered at Bachelor's Walk, killing three people and wounding over thirty. Many people in Dublin were enraged at these killings. Huge crowds attended the funerals of the victims and much support resulted for the Volunteers' cause. Éamonn Ceannt paid for the production of a brass memorial plaque to those killed. However, the British authorities would not allow the plaque to be erected and it was stolen sometime later.

Ceannt was also present on 1 August 1914 when 600 rifles and 11,500 rounds of ammunition were successfully landed at Kilcoole, County Wicklow. He had been acting as adjudicator at an Oireachtas piping competition when he was advised of the situation and he left immediately for Kilcoole.[1]

In an RTÉ interview in 1966, Bulmer Hobson said that after the Howth gun-running episode the Volunteers were receiving about £1,000 a month from America. In fact, between 1913 and 1916 Clan na Gael – the Irish-American organisation which had similar objectives to the IRB – sent a total of $100,000 to the IRB and the Volunteers. Hobson also said that Ceannt, whom he described as 'a brave, practical realist' was looking after the Volunteers' finances. He stated that only a small group of people knew of the financial arms deals as Ceannt was keeping the books in such a way that only a professional accountant could understand them. This was particularly useful as Redmond's people were taking their place in the Volunteer movement and the IRB were trying to avoid any detection of the arms they were bringing in. Ceannt's commitment to the Irish cause did not go unnoticed by the extreme republicans. In 1914, he was recruited to the supreme council of the IRB along with Patrick Pearse, Seán Mac Diarmada and Thomas Clarke.[2]

On 4 August 1914, Britain declared war on Germany. In his speech to the House of Commons the previous day, John Redmond suggested that Britain could safely withdraw her forces from Ireland and leave the defence of the country to the Irish Volunteers. However, this declaration was misinterpreted as a pledge of total Irish support for England's war effort and was met with great enthusiasm by an emotionally charged House of Commons. After the meeting, Redmond wrote to MacNeill explaining the situation and requesting his support; he ended by writing: 'Do not let us by our folly or temper destroy the situation.'

The outbreak of war changed the government's priorities and they suspended the implementation of home rule until at least after the war had ended. Redmond had agreed with the suspension of home rule and encouraged the Irish Volunteers to support England by enlisting for service. However, there was already growing concern and suspicion among the Volunteers over the home rule issue and many feared that it might never be implemented because of the strong opposition by Ulster's unionists. This promise of support by Redmond and the suspension of home rule eventually caused a split in the Irish camp. An estimated 170,000 men followed Redmond and became known as the National Volunteers, leaving Eoin MacNeill with only 10,000 Irish Volunteers.[3]

The nationalists lost no time in trying to reorganise. On 5 September 1914 it was agreed at a meeting of the IRB Supreme Council that a rebellion would take place and that they should accept any assistance that Germany would offer. Although no definite date was set for the rebellion, it was decided that any of the following reasons would prompt immediate action: if Germany invaded Ireland, if England tried to force conscription in Ireland, or if the war looked like it was coming to an end. It was also agreed that a declaration of war on Britain would accompany the insurrection. Having been contacted by William O'Brien of the Irish Citizen Army, Éamonn Ceannt arranged a nationalist conference for 9 September 1914. The meeting was held in the library of the Gaelic League offices at 25 Parnell Square. Those present included Tom Clarke, Seán Mac Diarmada, Joseph Plunkett, Patrick Pearse, Seán T. O'Kelly, John MacBride, Thomas MacDonagh, Arthur Griffith, James Connolly, William O'Brien and, of course, Éamonn Ceannt. There had been earlier disagreements between the IRB and the Citizen Army, but the outbreak of war in Europe changed the situation. Although the split had vastly reduced the Irish Volunteer numbers, the IRB members were not overly concerned as they believed that it would be easier to control a smaller organisation.

At the Volunteers' convention held in the Abbey Theatre on 25 October 1914, MacNeill remained as chairman with The O'Rahilly as treasurer, Joseph Plunkett as co-treasurer, Éamonn Ceannt as financial secretary, Patrick Pearse as press secretary and Bulmer Hobson as general secretary. The appointments of Ceannt, Pearse and Plunkett gave the IRB an even stronger position within the ranks of the Volunteers. These three men also formed the military committee of the IRB, which was founded to draw up plans for an insurrection.[4]

In February 1915 Ceannt assisted in the establishment of an Irish Volunteer Insurance Society, known as An Cumann Cosanta. The object of the society was to insure people involved with any Irish nationalist movement, but in particular the Irish Volunteers, against the loss of earnings consequent on their involvement. All nationalists, both men and women, were eligible for enrolment at the weekly subscription of 3d. The rules stated that no payments would be made to anyone who had been a member for less than eight weeks or who was four weeks or more in arrears. Neither would payment be made unless it was clearly established that the loss of earning was due to the claimant's connection with an Irish nationalist movement.[5]

8

Planning for Rebellion

On 10 March 1915, Éamonn Ceannt, Thomas MacDonagh, Edward Daly and Éamon de Valera were all promoted to the rank of commandant. By this time the Irish Volunteers were made up of a number of battalions, and Ceannt was placed in command of the Fourth Battalion. Each battalion comprised a commandant, vice-commandant, adjutant, quartermaster and six companies, A to F. Ceannt had already been appointed director of communications at an earlier general council meeting. At the same meeting, Joseph Plunkett had been appointed as director of military operations and Thomas MacDonagh was appointed as director of training. Ceannt and Plunkett were now in key positions – a perfect situation for the hard-line revolutionary camp. Ceannt's position was particularly beneficial as it allowed him to communicate with almost all officers in the field. By this time his public writings had become more patriotic and were sowing the seeds of unrest and revolution among young nationalists. The following is an example from *Spark* magazine of March 1915 of his passion for a new Ireland:

Ireland, too is at war – at war with Anglicisation … Eire, her heroes and heroines, must be the burden of our songs and choruses. The glories of our motherland, the valour of her sons, the virtue and beauty of her daughters – these themes for song in resurgent Ireland, and if we may not sing, if the bard be again proscribed, then let us watch – and pray. God save Ireland …

And when you realise that a country the size of Munster can make world-history, you will seriously ask why Ireland, the mother of heroes, is the Cinderella of the Nations. And while she is in rags and tatters, without arms, without language, without the right to rule her own household, you will see that, after all, there is more than meets the thinking Irishman's eye in the adjuration to remember Belgium.

The enemy is within our gates … Truly, Irishmen, ye do not sufficiently realise the importance of the war on which we are engaged. Ye do not know whose turn it may be next to fall. Then, in the language of the man with the ribbons enlist today in one of the gallant regiments which is fighting for the cause we have all at heart. Join the Irish Language Movement; motto: 'Remember Ireland!' Do not be a shirker. Ireland needs every son.[1]

In May 1915, the IRB military committee, which had lapsed for a time, reformed and later became the military council. Once again Pearse, Plunkett and Ceannt began putting together military plans for a rebellion. As the plans progressed, Thomas Clarke and Seán Mac Diarmada were recruited onto the military council. As director of communications, Ceannt was making personal, political and military contacts throughout Ireland. In his home county he had contacts in Athenry, Barna, Castlegar, Claregalway, Clifden, Spiddal, Maree, Oranmore and, of course, Galway city. He initiated a secret Irish Volunteer postal system called An Post Gaelach, which began on 15 November 1915. In order for this system to be successful, a number of 'safe houses' had to be established. The sender would leave the letter and a penny at the safe house. Then a courier would collect the letters plus money and deliver all letters within a certain radius of Dublin. If the courier failed to deliver any letter, it was returned to the point of collection. By charging the penny, it was hoped that the postal service would finance itself. Ceannt set up a similar postal system for delivery to various other counties.

At first the system required the couriers to record the time of departure and the time of arrival at their final destination. The courier also required a rough sketch map of the location to avoid attracting attention by asking for directions. In some cases the letter could be sent to a safe house by ordinary post and then redelivered to its final destination by courier. Letters which were not to be delivered by the ordinary postal system were marked 'By Hand Only'. Eventually the Volunteer post became very organised, with collection each night at 8 p.m. and delivery beginning at 8 a.m. the following morning. In order to avoid any confusion over the system, Ceannt drew up a brief but detailed step by step set of postal instructions.

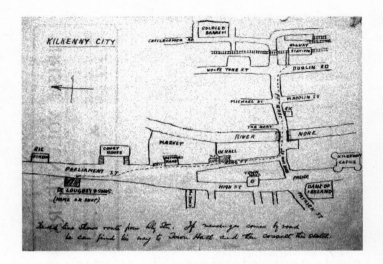

Example of a location map used by the Volunteer postal service, An Post Gaelach (*courtesy of the Allen Library*).

In an attempt to raise more funds for the Irish Volunteers Ceannt wrote the following song, 'Ireland Over All'. Copies of the song were on sale from Ceannt's house at 2 Dolphin Terrace and the profits went to the coffers of the Fourth Battalion. The air used for the song was 'Deutschland Über Alles':

Ireland, Ireland, 'fore the wide world,
Ireland, Ireland, over all;
When we fight we'll fight for Ireland,
Answer only Ireland's call;
Plain and mountain, rock and ocean,
From the Shannon to the sea;

Ireland, Ireland, 'fore the wide world,
Ireland one and Ireland free.

Ireland's land and Ireland's nation,
Ireland's faith and hope and song,
Irishmen will yet redeem them,
From the foreign tyrant throng;
Ireland's home and Ireland's hillsides,
Shall be freed from slavery,
Ireland, Ireland, 'fore the wide world,
Ireland one and Ireland free.

Unity and right and freedom,
For our Irish fatherland,
Strive we all we may secure them,
Strive we all with heart and hand;
Be our aim, them God defending,
Right, eternal liberty;
Ireland, Ireland, 'fore the wide world,
Ireland one and Ireland free.[2]

On 1 August 1915, the funeral of the old Fenian, Jeremiah O'Donovan Rossa, took place in Glasnevin Cemetery in Dublin. Patrick Pearse, dressed in the full uniform of the Irish Volunteers, delivered the oration. It was Pearse's greatest test, and before a gathering of thousands he rose to the occasion. The following extract shows just how intense the political situation had become:

Life springs from death; and from the graves of patriot men

and women spring living nations ... They think that they have foreseen everything, think that they have provided against everything; but the fools, the fools, the fools! – they have left us our Fenian dead, and while Ireland holds these graves, Ireland unfree shall never be at peace.

Listening to the fire in Pearse's words, those present were under no illusion as to what lay ahead. Although the British authorities knew most of the dangerous men, they were still in an impossible dilemma. By now reports of heavy casualties were flooding in from the Western Front and were beginning to change Irish enthusiasm for the war effort. In addition, the anti-enlistment campaign by the separatists was also having an effect. The nationalists were armed and the authorities knew that they could not be suppressed without massive bloodshed, but neither could they be ignored.[3]

Little did Ceannt realise that when he crossed the River Shannon in August 1915 to where his heart lay in the west that it would be his final visit to Galway and Spiddal. Áine and Rónán accompanied him and they stayed with Michael Thornton near Spiddal. His days were spent wandering along the beach and walking in the mountains. During the evening and night he trained and advised the local Volunteers in the use of guns and drill. On other evenings he entertained the locals by playing the pipes at various houses. He also spent some time at the Irish College. One evening, while he was returning from the college to Spiddal with a friend, the constabulary stopped them because they had no lamps on their bicycles. When asked his name Éamonn answered in Irish as he did all their questions which caused confusion and annoyance for the police as they did not understand him. A few days later he received a summons and a month later found himself in court. Although he was penalised he never paid the fine.

One day while walking along Spiddal beach with Michael Thornton he found a bullet. Picking it up he asked Michael if he knew what it was but before he could answer, Ceannt continued by saying, 'When the Rising is about to start I will ask you again.' To which Michael answered, 'OK, but you send us some guns.' By the end of his stay Ceannt was leaving behind a confident Volunteer company in Galway, eager and full of anticipation for the future.[4]

In January 1916 the IRB military council began holding their meetings at Ceannt's house at Dolphin's Barn. Áine remembers seeing Tom Clarke, Patrick Pearse and Seán Mac Diarmada at the first meeting and, although she had no recollection of Joseph Plunkett, she was sure he must have attended. One of the issues on the agenda was the Conscription Act which came into force in England on 16 January 1916. The question now was: what effect would this have on Ireland? If it were introduced in Ireland it would be a signal for rebellion.

At the time, James Connolly, who knew nothing of the rebellion being planned, was getting impatient and was calling for action, saying, 'The time for Ireland's battle is

NOW, the place for Ireland's battle is HERE.' He was also using the phrase, 'England's difficulty is Ireland's opportunity.' It was clear that he was contemplating a rebellion with the Irish Citizen Army. This worried the IRB military council because any such action could undermine their plans. It was crucial that Connolly be brought into their confidence. Thomas Clarke and Seán Mac Diarmada persuaded Connolly to attend a meeting with the IRB military council on 19 January. Following the meeting Connolly disappeared. Ceannt was greatly concerned. While at home that evening, Áine jokingly asked Ceannt for a few pounds before the rebellion started. Ceannt replied, 'It might start sooner than you expect, James Connolly has disappeared.' He added that Connolly had left orders with his second-in-command that if at any time he should disappear and had not returned within three days, then the Irish Citizen Army should attack Dublin Castle. Ceannt continued by saying, 'We can't let the Citizen Army go out alone; if they go out we must go with them.' A deputation went to meet with the leadership of the Citizen Army requesting them not to do anything hasty and to wait a few more days. Ceannt sent orders to all officers of the Fourth Battalion to report to him immediately. He told them that he was going out to check the results of the meeting with Connolly's men and said that upon his return they would either receive orders for ordinary manoeuvres or for action. However, Connolly later surfaced and any immediate action was avoided.[5]

Connolly was present at the following military council meeting held in Ceannt's house and it may have been at this meeting that he was sworn into the IRB and then drafted onto the military council. A date for the insurrection was set: Easter Sunday, 23 April 1916.

In February the military council made contact with John Devoy, one of the most influential leaders of Clan na Gael in America. Devoy notified the German authorities of the IRB's plans and advised them to send arms to Ireland for arrival on Good Friday or Easter Saturday. On 9 March the IRB received confirmation that a consignment of 20,000 German rifles and 10 machine guns would arrive off the County Kerry coast between 23 and 25 April. No one outside the military council and the leaders of Clan na Gael knew when the action was going to take place.

Volunteers were already beginning to arrive back from England, among them Michael Collins, who took temporary work at the Plunkett home in Larkfield, Kimmage. Larkfield was to be the headquarters of the Fourth Battalion, but it also became the general headquarters for the company of Volunteers who were returning from England for the rebellion. This special unit worked closely with the Fourth Battalion and it was in the pleasant surroundings of Larkfield that the everyday business of the Volunteers was carried out. Apart from intensive drilling, the main activity was rifle practice and manufacturing munitions, including bayonets and even pikes.[6]

On St Patrick's Day 1916, the Dublin battalions of

the Irish Volunteers assembled at College Green. They planned to attend a special military mass which was to be held in Ss Michael and John's Church at 9 a.m. Ceannt's Fourth Battalion served the mass and provided the guard of honour. After the mass the Volunteers, complete with rifles and fixed bayonets, marched to College Green where Eoin MacNeill inspected them. Martin Daly later recalled that Ceannt was in full Volunteer uniform marching at the head of his men. They spoke a few words in Irish. Martin said, 'A great day for Ireland', and Ceannt replied, 'Let us hope so.' Áine also went to see the assembled Volunteers and viewed the scene from the top of a tramcar near the statue of King William III at College Green. While sitting there she noticed another interested party, Viscount Powerscourt, who was appointed provost marshal immediately after the rebellion. He was intently watching the proceedings but obviously for very different reasons. After inspection the various battalions returned to their headquarters.[7]

Shortly before holy week, Thomas MacDonagh joined the military council. The council was now complete with its seven members and it was these men who made the final decision that the only way Ireland would gain its independence was through the blood sacrifice of an armed struggle.

Just over a week before the planned rebellion, Liam Mellows arrived back from England disguised as a priest. Mellows was born in Lancashire in 1892 where his father, a British soldier, was stationed at the time. The family had moved to Dublin while Mellows was still a child. As a young man, Mellows became very involved in Irish affairs and in 1913 joined the IRB. The following year he took command of the Volunteers in south Galway. In March 1916, Mellows had been arrested at Athenry, County Galway and was sent to Arbour Hill Barracks to await deportation to England. Mellows was vital to the Galway rebellion and the IRB needed to be aware of his location if he was sent to England. So every few days Áine visited Mrs Mellows after she had returned from visiting her son in Arbour Hill and was then able to inform Ceannt of any movement from the prison without drawing much attention. Eventually the authorities arranged to have Mellows placed with relatives in Leek in England. His movements would be restricted and he would be kept under constant surveillance. Upon receiving the information, the IRB acted immediately and set about their plan to have him returned to Ireland. The strategy involved his brother, Barney Mellows, who bore a striking resemblance to Liam, and James Connolly's daughter, Nora. Barney and Nora were sent to England to make contact with Liam. When Barney reached the house where Liam was staying, both men retired to one of the bedrooms where they switched clothes. In the coat pocket Liam found a ferry ticket to Ireland and detailed instructions on what to do when he arrived in Dublin. Liam then went to meet Nora and the return journey took them back through Glasgow where Liam was supplied with clerical clothing. Upon reaching Dublin it had been arranged that he should stay with the Ceannts, but it seems that Ceannt had doubts about this idea as he did not wish to draw any unnecessary attention so close to the rebellion. Mellows was then placed for a short time at the home of Volunteer Frank Fahy in Cunningham Road. Barney remained in England long enough to secure Liam's escape and then returned to Ireland by a different route.[8]

Just prior to the rising, Martin Daly met Ceannt for the last time in the Antient Concert Rooms where a huge meeting was taking place. During the meeting the vast audience reacted angrily to some political speeches being made and began yelling and shouting. The fiery response from the hall prompted Ceannt to gather his pipes at the interval and, rising before the audience, he began to play in the hope of calming the situation. Daly later recorded his last memories of Ceannt as he played before the crowd:

> … and even then, not foreseeing even dimly how soon the desperate effort, the tragic end, was coming, even then I felt very sharply, like a knife slashing between my bones, that he stood in some quite rare way as the symbol of his times. So gravely, so religiously piping, piping as it were without enthusiasm, as a duty, as a solemn declaration of faith, almost ritually, he appeared before my mind as a grave ghost of the old Ireland rising to haunt the new and to awe it into homage and obedience.

9

Holy Week

On Palm Sunday, Ceannt returned from a meeting of the Volunteers which Áine believed was an executive meeting. He told her that in the event of a successful outcome to the rebellion they had to discuss the various posts which each of them should hold in a new government, adding: 'Personally, I was very pleased that I was chosen to be Minister for War.' Áine asked him about other appointments, including Éamon de Valera, to which he replied: 'Oh, he says he'll go down in the fight, whereas Tomás MacDonagh says that he will come through, as he always falls on his feet.' Áine then asked Ceannt how long he expected the fighting to last, to which he replied: 'If we last more than a month we will have won.' At this point Áine still had no knowledge of the actual date of the Rising. That same night the Ceannts received an invitation to a ceilidhe from Captain George Irvine of the Fourth Battalion to be held on Saturday 29 April. Áine was hoping to attend and asked Ceannt if they should go, to which he replied vaguely: 'Perhaps.' During the previous week there had been several false alarms in the city and because of this Ceannt was refusing to attend social events; he did not wish to be out of touch with the likelihood of military raids and the seizure of arms.[1]

On the Monday of Holy Week Ceannt informed Áine that he was taking a week's holidays from work, saying that he did not wish to be 'caught like a rat in a trap'. He suggested that they should take little Rónán and visit the Pearse family at St Enda's, which was closed for the holidays. When they arrived they were sent to the garden at the rear of the building. In the distance, coming through a vista of trees, they noticed a young cleric approaching. As he drew near there were smiles all round and shortly they were clasping the hand of Liam Mellows in his priestly disguise. Mrs Pearse and her son Patrick then joined them. While the men chatted, Áine and Mrs Pearse admired the greenhouses and went to look at the Sarah Curran tree, named after Robert Emmet's sweetheart. Soon lunch was announced and they all went into the dining-room. Patrick's brother, William, and his sister, Margaret, also joined them. They had a pleasant meal, the conversation roaming from books to music and other interests, but there was no mention of impending rebellion. After lunch, Áine took Rónán by the hand and bade goodbye to their hosts. She would never see the two Pearse brothers alive again. Áine and Rónán went for a walk in the front grounds of St Enda's while Ceannt discussed the events of the coming week with the others. For Áine, the wait in the grounds seemed like an eternity but at last Ceannt appeared and they started for home. It was only then that Áine began to fully realise the importance of their visit. Ceannt asked Áine if she would accompany Liam Mellows' mother to St Enda's that night so that she might say goodbye to Liam as he had orders to leave for Galway the following day.[2]

On Tuesday Ceannt went to Mount Pleasant Square to meet with Seán Fitzgibbon. Fitzgibbon had been ordered to travel south to rendezvous with the southern Volunteers and await the arrival of Roger Casement with the German arms shipment. When Ceannt returned home, he told Áine of a secret document which Alderman Tom Kelly was to read before Dublin Corporation during proceedings the following day. The document supposedly contained orders from a British general to raid all the Volunteer premises in Dublin. Although it was a forgery, Áine believes that Ceannt never doubted the authenticity of the document. That night, while undressing for bed, Ceannt took a Mauser pistol and placed it beside his bed, remarking to Áine, 'We are living in stirring times.' As Áine watched him in silence, he continued, 'If we live through this night we will have drawn first blood.' Ceannt felt that if the British were going to make their move, then it would be that night, as it was their last chance before the document was read. It was a restless night for both of them and with the coming of dawn, Áine thanked God that the night had passed peacefully.[3]

Wednesday was an exceptionally wet day and Ceannt left home early for meetings. Áine took Rónán with her into the city to buy a knapsack and some supplies for the coming manoeuvres. When she returned there were two Volunteers with Ceannt who had been ordered to meet with Seán Fitzgibbon in Kerry. Áine believes that they travelled south to Tralee the next day. It was a busy day in Volunteer circles. Another meeting was held in the city, after which several Volunteers called to Ceannt's house to speak with him. Áine learned later that these men were couriers who were being sent throughout the country with instructions for the coming rebellion. Ceannt was trying to ensure that when the Volunteers in Dublin went into action they would not be alone.

Late that evening, while Bulmer Hobson, a former IRB council member, was still working at his office in Dawson Street, he received the startling news of the impending rebellion. Two prominent Volunteers arrived and informed him that several battalions outside Dublin had received orders for a rebellion on Easter Sunday. The three men went immediately to MacNeill's home at Woodtown Park, Rathfarnham. MacNeill was furious that his authority as chief-of-staff had been undermined and, although it was after midnight, he insisted that Hobson accompany him to St Enda's to see Pearse. Pearse confirmed that a rising was intended and that it had been necessary to keep such plans as quiet as possible. MacNeill flew into a temper and showered Pearse with verbal abuse and, before leaving, told him that there would be no waste of lives for which he was directly responsible. He said that short of informing

Dublin Castle, he would do everything in his power to stop the rebellion and then, waving his fist angrily at Pearse, he stormed out. MacNeill may have suspected earlier than this that a rising was being planned, because on 5 April he had insisted that all orders were to be countersigned by him.

On the morning of Good Friday, Pearse, Mac Diarmada and MacDonagh went to speak with MacNeill to try and convince him to join the rebellion. MacNeill would only speak with Mac Diarmada, who convinced him that German guns were about to be landed in Kerry and that a rebellion was inevitable. Even if they cancelled it, the authorities would definitely disarm the Volunteers and arrest the leaders if they learned of the arms landing. MacNeill agreed to go into action with them and went down to meet with the others. When he entered the drawing-room he at once approached Pearse and shook his hand; all present then sat down to breakfast.[4]

Meanwhile in County Kerry, Roger Casement, Robert Monteith of the IRB and Sergeant Daniel Bailey of the Royal Irish Rifles had landed at Banna Strand in the early hours. Bailey had been in a German prisoner-of-war camp and was released to join the Irish Brigade which Casement had tried to set up using Irish prisoners-of-war, but without much success. The three men had arrived off the Irish coast in a German submarine and were trying to come ashore in a small collapsible boat when it capsized. They eventually made it to the beach, where Monteith and

Bailey went to seek help, while Casement remained close to the strand. However, a local man raised the alarm, the police arrived, and a number of hours later Casement was arrested and taken to Ardfert. The *Aud*, which was carrying the arms and the hopes of a successful revolt, also arrived off the Kerry coast. However, the ship was intercepted by two British warships and escorted towards Queenstown (Cobh). At the entrance to Cork Harbour, Captain Karl Spindler ordered that the ship be scuttled, sending the much-needed arms to the bottom of the sea.

That afternoon in Dublin the Ceannt family attended Good Friday devotions. During the prayers, Áine observed a Volunteer as he entered the church. He scanned the congregation until he located Ceannt, then walked directly towards him and, upon reaching him, bent over and whispered something in his ear. He then left the church. Ceannt showed no expression and made no comment at the time. Later that evening he and Áine went for a walk in the Phoenix Park. It was a fine evening and they sat on a bench overlooking the river with their backs to the magazine fort, which held the British arsenal in the park. They sat mainly in silence and Áine noticed that there was a continuous stream of lorries leaving the fort. She also noted that Ceannt had very little to say, and later the only remark she could remember him making, was: 'You can almost over-organise things.'[5]

10

Mobilisation

On Saturday morning at breakfast, Áine drew Ceannt's attention to a report in the newspaper. It concerned the arrival of a collapsible boat off the Kerry coast and the arrest of what she termed 'a strange man'. Ceannt made no comment so Áine did not pursue the matter. That evening The O'Rahilly brought two Volunteer officers to meet with MacNeill and give him the news of the sinking of the *Aud*. MacNeill went immediately to see Pearse in a vain attempt to have the rebellion called off. Later that night MacNeill issued orders calling off the planned rebellion. The O'Rahilly, who was also against the rebellion, began a tour of various counties issuing MacNeill's countermanding orders:

Woodtown Park
Rathfarnham
Co. Dublin
22 April, 1916
Volunteers completely deceived. All orders for special action are hereby cancelled, and on no account will action be taken.

Signed Eoin MacNeill,
Chief of Staff.

Other Volunteers were sent by train and taxi to various
parts of the country with the same orders. Arthur Griffith, who was also strongly opposed to the rebellion, had
spent all day Saturday issuing MacNeill's countermanding
orders to commanders in the Dublin area. Griffith was now
undermining the orders directed by Ceannt. During that
day MacNeill had also prepared a similar statement for the
Sunday Independent and to make sure that it was published,
he delivered it personally to the editor. Ceannt was, as yet,
unaware of these countermanding orders. The statement
read:

> Owing to the very critical position, all orders given to the
> Irish Volunteers for Easter Sunday are hereby rescinded, and
> no parades, marches or other movements of Irish Volunteers
> will take place.[1]

After breakfast that morning the Ceannts went to Dalkey
to visit the Washington family and Ceannt borrowed a pair
of binoculars from them. During the tram journey Ceannt
turned and whispered to Áine, 'The man who landed in
Kerry was Roger Casement and the man who got away
was Monteith. If they catch Monteith they'll hang him.'
This was the message which Ceannt had received while at
devotions the previous day. Áine had never questioned her
husband on his political beliefs or activities, knowing that

when the time was right he would always enlighten her. Ceannt had, over recent months, tried not to burden or worry Áine and would only inform her of certain situations when he felt it was necessary. The couple stayed for lunch in Dalkey but nothing would persuade Ceannt to remain later than 4 p.m. He was very anxious to return, saying that he had an important appointment. At about 6 p.m. Ceannt told Áine that they had planned the rebellion for the following day and that his headquarters would be in the South Dublin Union. This would prove to be the scene of some of the most bitter fighting in the rebellion. He told her that there were rumours of a secret session of the British parliament and that it could mean conscription. He went on to say that, as an armed body of men, they could not let this opportunity pass without striking a blow while England was at war, adding that they would be a disgrace to their generation if they did not act. He then informed her that he would not be staying at home that night for security reasons. After evening tea Ceannt wrote letters to his brothers, Richard and Michael, which were delivered the following day through the Volunteer postal service. The contents of both letters were very similar:

To Master Michael and family with best Easter wishes. All well here – on the defensive. If the friends of the small nationalities should decide on interfering with our Inspections tomorrow I would advise you to make yourselves scarce. Your own house is the safest place from 4 p.m., our hour of assembly, until such time as the danger of an attack

is passed, which would be about 7 p.m. Come what may we
are ready.
Éamonn Ceannt.
22/4/1916.

Having completed his correspondence, he prepared to
go to church for confession. As he left the house, he told
them that he would not be long as he was expecting Lily to
deliver a tricolour flag which Mrs Mellows had made and
which one of the Volunteer officers was going to collect.
Ceannt was still out when Lily arrived, but upon returning
from church he greeted all those present and went to
examine the flag. It was then sprinkled with 'Easter (Holy)
Water'. Later that night Phil Cosgrave, who Áine believed
was a battalion quartermaster, called to see Ceannt. Before
leaving, Ceannt asked him to take the flag with him and
jokingly said to him: 'Be sure and turn out the green side.'[2]

Ceannt then left for his safe-house but returned
shortly afterwards having changed his mind about staying
away from home that night. If it was to be his last night
on earth, he was going to spend it with his wife and child.
Before retiring, Áine asked Ceannt if the men under
his command knew the position. He told her that the
Volunteers in his battalion had been warned repeatedly
that some day they would go out and not return, but added
that he could not risk informing them of the rebellion. He
went on to say that all the commanders were fully aware
of the situation.

According to Áine, there was an attempt by the Volunteer leadership to possibly win over at least one of the IRB leaders. It seems that after the order cancelling manoeuvres had actually been issued to the newspaper, the Volunteer leadership summoned Thomas MacDonagh to a meeting. During the meeting, MacNeill asked him for his opinion on the matter. MacDonagh looked round the room and replied: 'I owe no counsel to these men.' He then left the house and went to see Cathal Brugha, Ceannt's second-in-command, and informed him of what had happened. Brugha went first to speak with MacNeill, but he became very angry when MacNeill would not change his decision not to be involved in the rebellion. After this meeting, Brugha went to speak with Ceannt, who by this time had gone to collect his equipment. Áine had gone to bed at twelve o'clock but was disturbed about two hours later by loud knocking at the hall door. Fearing that the authorities had been alarmed, she opened the top window and looked out. A voice in the darkness asked for Ceannt in Irish and she knew it was Cathal Brugha. Áine told him where he would locate Ceannt and without another word he went away. Within half an hour Ceannt returned with all his equipment, guns, ammunition, etc. Ceannt told Áine that he would have to go out again, saying: 'MacNeill has ruined us – he has stopped the Rising.' Áine was astonished and started to make suggestions, but Ceannt replied: 'The countermanding order is already in the hands of the newspaper. I'm off now to see if anything can be done.'[3]

Ceannt went first to try to locate MacNeill but failed to do so. His next stop was James Connolly who was in Liberty Hall, but the armed guard refused to disturb Connolly. From there he went to the Metropole Hotel, where Joseph Plunkett was staying. Plunkett had also left word that he was not to be disturbed under any circumstances until 9 a.m. It was 5 a.m. when Ceannt returned home and told Áine that he had failed to make contact with anyone. She prepared some hot milk for him and he went up to the bedroom. The bell for the angelus was striking as he lay down and, turning to Áine, he said: 'If I sleep now I would sleep on dynamite.' At about 7 a.m. on Easter Sunday morning a courier arrived with a letter for Ceannt from Liberty Hall. Áine went quietly to the bedroom but, as Ceannt was still sleeping soundly, she decided not to disturb him. She felt that at this stage he needed to rest as he would have serious decisions to make during the day. She placed the letter beside his bed where he would see it the moment he opened his eyes. Mrs Mellows called on her way to 8 a.m. mass and Áine told her of the pending rebellion and asked her to pray for the men. At 8.30 a.m. Captain Séamus Murphy of the Fourth Battalion called and said that it was important that he speak to the commandant. Áine said that he had been out most of the night but, when Murphy insisted, she went and called Ceannt. He came down immediately with the letter in his hand and spoke for a few minutes with Captain Murphy, who then left. Turning to Áine, he asked how long the dispatch had been in the house. When she told him over an hour he immediately took his bicycle and without waiting for breakfast or even donning a collar and tie, he departed for Liberty Hall. The letter was from James Connolly summoning him to a meeting to decide a plan of action now that it was too late to stop the countermanding orders. The letter read: 'MacDonagh and I agree that it is important we have a conference immediately as various messengers are awaiting a decision. Seamus.'[4]

As the morning wore on, Volunteers of the Fourth Battalion besieged the house, all seeking an explanation of the countermanding orders they had just read in the morning newspaper. Áine could give them no information, merely saying that the commandant had been called out early and suggested that they should await his return. Soon the drawing-room was uncomfortably filled and the bicycles were stacked four deep in the front garden. To pass the time Captain Douglas fFrench Mullen, who was a fine pianist, played some tunes; one of the airs he chose was 'The Dead March'. Ceannt's brother and sister, Michael and Nell, arrived and forced an entry into the already packed house. Michael noticed all the bicycles and upon seeing Ceannt's young dispatch riders, commented: 'Look what's going to free Ireland!'

At about 1 p.m. Ceannt returned and had a meeting with the men. He instructed them not to leave the city and that if they left home, even to go for a walk, they were to state where they could be located at short notice. Ceannt then went to collect a Volunteer journal in the back room where the family had gathered. He was now in excellent humour, until Michael told him that their Aunt Liz had just died. He looked a little shocked at first but continued with the business at hand, preparing to issue the latest orders to those who were still arriving at the house. A short time later, Michael, Nell and Lily decided to return to their own homes. Upon returning home, Michael began writing a letter to Ceannt appealing to him to resign from the Volunteers. Michael feared for Ceannt's safety and also believed that physical force against England was utter madness. He wanted to tell Ceannt that, as with other hobbies in his life, he would tire of this and wanted him to do so now before it was too late. He later admitted, however, that he knew that once Ceannt felt that there was even a small chance of striking a serious blow for Ireland 'wild horses would not pull him back'.[5]

After dinner Ceannt suggested that Áine accompany him to Howth. She later recalled him standing silently, staring out from the pier, where two years earlier the famous gun-running episode had taken place. They returned home and, after evening tea, Ceannt said he was going to use the front room for Volunteer business. Áine asked if there was anything she could do to help. He at once said yes and pushed a bundle of mobilisation orders to be completed towards her saying: 'Oh, I forgot to tell you we strike tomorrow – write in Emerald Square, 11 o'clock.' When this task was completed, she went to a neighbouring house, the home of the MacCarthy family, where she requested couriers. On her way she met a young woman, Millie Keegan, who was going to evening devotions. Clutching Áine, she said, 'Oh, what does it mean – Ned got orders to stay near home and he wouldn't even come for a walk with us.' Áine told her to 'pray hard' as there was going to be a lot of trouble but dared not tell her that her husband would be in action the following day. When she arrived at MacCarthy's house there was a bit of a sing-song going on. Dan MacCarthy told Áine that they were expecting her, adding that the men were 'standing-to' and would leave immediately to meet with Ceannt. Áine had scarcely returned home when the couriers arrived. They were given their dispatches and then departed for their various destinations. After the couriers had left, Áine began to discuss the overall effect the countermanding orders would have on the rebellion and the fact that they had placed Ceannt in an extremely difficult position. He felt under the circumstances that all had been done that could have been done to ensure the rebellion went ahead. He was also sure this was the safest night to stay at home: 'I may thank John (Eoin) MacNeill that I can sleep in my own house – the cancelling of the manoeuvres will lead the British to believe that everything is all right.'[6]

As Easter Monday, 24 April 1916, dawned, the Ceannt home was a hive of activity. While dressing, Áine asked Ceannt how long he expected the fighting to last and could he depend on the country, to which he replied, 'If

we last a month they – the British – will come to terms.'
As for a countrywide rebellion, he had already issued new
orders, but felt that because of the conflicting orders the
Volunteer commanders had received over the past two
days it was difficult to know what was going to happen,
but he added, 'I have made sure of Galway, where the finest
men in Ireland are.' His message to Mellows was 'Dublin
is now in action!' Before leaving the bedroom he told Áine
not to worry: 'We will put our trust in God.'

Soon there was a constant stream of men coming to
and going from the house in the morning sunshine. Áine
remembered seeing Barney Mellows before he went to
the Phoenix Park where he was to join a number of other
Volunteers for the attack on the magazine fort. It was their
job to blow up the magazine fort, and this was to signal the
beginning of hostilities. Two messages arrived from Cathal
Brugha, one advising Ceannt of the small turnout and
asking what time he should leave. The *Irish Independent*
that morning repeated a call from MacNeill that 'no
parades, marches, or other movements of Irish Volunteers
will take place', making the situation for the rebels even
worse. Ceannt was already dressed in his uniform and, after
the last Volunteers had left the house, he sent the final
dispatches. Áine's sister Lily had also got her mobilisation
orders and would be attached to the Fourth Battalion.
Ceannt had made arrangements earlier for Áine, Rónán
and Áine's mother to stay at Cathal Brugha's house. The
Brughas had kindly placed rooms at their disposal, and

items of food and clothing had already been sent there. Ceannt believed that their own house would be in the line of fire and could be a possible target for the enemy.[7]

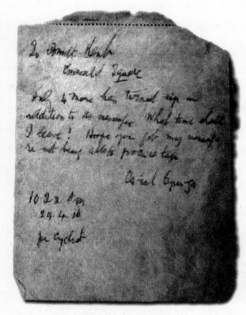

Second letter from Cathal Brugha to Éamonn Ceannt, Easter Monday 1916 (*courtesy of the Allen Library*).

When Áine's mother, who was living with them at the time, returned from 8 a.m. mass, she was told that she would have to leave home immediately after breakfast, along with Áine and Rónán. She flatly refused to move, making all kinds of excuses. Áine told her that her clothes had already been sent to the other house, but did not waste time arguing. It was now time for Ceannt to leave and he gathered his equipment, including his gun and a large bag of ammunition. Áine helped him to put on his Sam Browne belt and then adjusted his knapsack, which was exceptionally large. He hugged and kissed Rónán goodbye and then Áine's mother took the child into another room to let Áine say farewell to her husband alone. Áine wanted to go to the rendezvous at Emerald Square and watch the men march off, but Ceannt asked her not to attend. She then embraced him lovingly in silence, both fully aware of the seriousness of the embrace. It was about fifteen minutes to eleven when he left to join his battalion. Rónán ran to the open door and his last memories of his father were of him walking away from the house wearing an Australian bushranger's hat, slouched on one side.[8]

Áine's next task was to get her mother and the child safely away. Although her mother was still protesting, Áine persuaded her to put on her coat and prepare to leave. Taking a basket of food, she then ushered her mother and little son into the empty street. She knew that this house would never mean home again and, closing the door, she said farewell to eleven years of happily married life. As they left Dolphin Terrace, Áine carried with her all that they possessed in the way of food. All the money they had in the world was in her pocket and she wore two dresses. Knowing that the rebellion would start at midday, it was important that they reach Mrs Brugha's house before the hostilities began. In order to catch the required trams, they had to cross the Grand Canal. They did so via Sally's Bridge, and as they crossed Áine observed British soldiers at the rear of

Wellington Barracks and wondered if they had any idea of what was about to happen. As they made their way along by the old Greenmount oil works, they met four or five Volunteers strolling along in uniform with full equipment. After a number of tram journeys, they finally reached their destination, arriving at Mrs Brugha's house in Fitzwilliam Terrace where they were at once made welcome.[9]

Shortly after Áine and her family arrived, Mrs Brugha's sister, Miss Kingston, came to the house. She had been attending a hospital on the other side of the city. The first comment she made was: 'I heard the shots.' At about 1 p.m., Miss Kingston and Áine decided to go out and buy some food in the local shops. They met a man with whom they were acquainted and, although he was a Volunteer, he was cycling fast away from the city. They stopped him, seeking news of the rebellion but the first words he uttered were: 'Davey's is blew up.' Davey's was a public house at the corner of Richmond Street at Portobello Bridge, from which one could apparently command the approach of troops from Portobello Barracks. Áine asked him what he meant but he did not answer her question and carried on, telling them that he was leaving the area. Miss Kingston said, 'Will you not wait and give a hand to your comrades?' to which he replied, 'Not likely. I'm getting away.' On that note they parted company and the women went and secured as many supplies as possible before returning to the Brugha household, which would be their home until the rebellion was over.[10]

11

A Terrible Beauty is Born

On Easter Monday morning a party of Irish Volunteers, joined by men from the Irish Citizen Army, assembled at Liberty Hall. The O'Rahilly, who had spent the previous days trying to prevent the rebellion, now joined the rebels at Liberty Hall, saying to Pearse: 'Well, I've helped to wind up the clock – I might as well hear it strike.' Under the command of Patrick Pearse, Thomas Clarke, James Connolly, Seán Mac Diarmada and Joseph Plunkett, the combined Irish forces then marched from Liberty Hall to the General Post Office (GPO) in Sackville Street in Dublin. Upon arrival at the GPO the rebels immediately occupied the building. As the panic-stricken staff and customers fled, Michael Collins took the rebellion's first prisoners, a British officer and an elderly policeman. Two Irish flags replaced the two British flags that flew over the building. One of the Irish flags was green with a gold harp in the centre and bore the words 'Irish Republic' in gold and white lettering, and the other was the tricolour.

When Pearse and Connolly emerged from the GPO to

declare Irish independence, a very concerned young bride staying at a nearby hotel observed them. Geraldine Plunkett had a special interest in the events now unfolding as she had three brothers in the GPO. The previous day, Geraldine and Thomas Dillon had married and had planned on a double wedding with Joseph Plunkett and Grace Gifford. However, owing to the circumstances, her brother's marriage had been postponed.

Patrick Pearse, commander-in-chief of the rebels, stood on the low step of the building inside the massive portico and unrolled the declaration of independence. A sudden hush fell over the street as he began to read aloud the Proclamation of the Irish Republic. When he finished reading, James Connolly stepped forward and shook his hand saying, 'Thanks be to God, Pearse, that we've lived to see this day.'

As was the case with The O'Rahilly, Arthur Griffith's opposition to the rebellion did not prevent him from trying to take his place in the ranks with the rebels now in control of the GPO. Reports are unclear on his movements during the rebellion, but it seems that upon hearing of the rebellion on Easter Monday, Griffith offered his services either by sending word or going himself to the rebel headquarters at the GPO. His offer was refused, however, on the grounds that if the Rising was to fail he would be more valuable to Ireland alive. Seán Mac Diarmada felt that his propaganda work was vital to the future of the movement and that those in the building were already committed.

Over the following five days, the GPO became the

headquarters of the Provisional Government of Ireland. At the time most people frowned on this act of rebellion. However, later it managed to wake a spirit of Irish nationalism, the effects of which can still be felt today. To ensure that the general public knew the reason for the rebellion, copies of the Proclamation were handed out to civilians. Other copies were posted on various buildings. Many years later, it was indicated that the handwriting on the original Proclamation manuscript was that of either Pearse or Ceannt, although the document appears to be mainly the work of Pearse, with input from Connolly and perhaps MacDonagh.

Just a few minutes after noon, Dublin Castle came under attack when a section of the Irish Citizen Army marched to the establishment. Upon reaching the gates, they were confronted by Constable James O'Brien who they immediately shot dead. They then forced the military to surrender the guardhouse but failed to press forward the attack. At this point, the castle was almost entirely at the mercy of the rebels as less than twenty-five soldiers protected it, though the rebels were unaware of this. Had they succeeded in capturing Dublin Castle it would have been an epic moment in Irish history. Instead they occupied other buildings in the area, including the *Evening Mail* offices and city hall, which overlooked the castle.

By now hostilities were breaking out all across the city. The First Battalion under Commandant Edward Daly occupied the Four Courts. He also set up a number of outposts, including the Mendicity Institution, where Seán Heuston, a young Volunteer officer, was placed in command. Barricades were then erected at Church Street and the surrounding area. Shortly afterwards, British Lancers of the Sixth Cavalry Reserve Regiment arrived on the scene. They were returning to Marlborough Barracks at the Phoenix Park with a small consignment of ammunition when they encountered Daly's men near the Four Courts. The Volunteers at the Church Street barricades immediately opened fire, hitting six or seven Lancers. Daly himself took part in the action, shooting one of the Lancers as he tried to get away. The surprised Lancers took evasive action but not without sustaining some casualties.[1]

About this time across the River Liffey, Éamonn Ceannt's sister, Nell, was making her way home to Drumcondra when she became fully aware of the seriousness of her brother's position. Upon arriving at Christchurch Place she was stopped by Volunteers who had taken control of a number of bridges over the Liffey. When she told them who she was, they allowed her through. One of them asked if she wished to see Ceannt and gestured towards the Four Courts. Nell assumed that he meant that Ceannt was in the Four Courts which, of course, was not the case. This confusion was most likely caused by the fact that a number of Volunteers from the Fourth Battalion had reported for duty at the Four Courts, while several others who were also unable to join their own units went into action at Church Street. However, Nell declined the offer.[2]

Commandant Michael Mallin and his second-in-command, Countess Markievicz, led a section of the Irish Citizen Army into St Stephen's Green. Action began as the rebels were taking control of the Green; the countess shot a police constable attempting to enter the park after he had refused to leave the area. Mallin then had barricades erected in the surrounding streets. He made no attempt to occupy the Shelbourne Hotel which would have given him a commanding view of the street, an error he later regretted. Instead the British took over the hotel and, after some sharp exchanges, forced Mallin to retreat to the College of Surgeons.

Éamon de Valera was in command of the Third Battalion of Irish Volunteers and took control of Boland's Mills. Other areas under de Valera's control were the railway line from Lansdowne Road to Westland Row. He also set up a number of outposts at Northumberland Road, Grand Canal Road and South Lotts Road.

Thomas MacDonagh and the Second Battalion occupied Jacob's Factory. He had outposts set up in the surrounding buildings and occupied positions in the Fairview–Ballybough area. Action began for MacDonagh just before 1 p.m. when Volunteers who had taken up positions at Camden Street prematurely opened fire on a small advance party of British military who were making their way to Dublin Castle. Although an officer and six men were hit, an opportunity to inflict heavier casualties was lost.

During the week some of the most ferocious fighting took place at Mount Street Bridge. Seven Volunteers under George Reynolds had occupied Clanwilliam House, which overlooked the bridge. Although facing overwhelming odds, they managed to inflict severe casualties on the British battalions. The commander of the British forces in Ireland, General Sir John Maxwell, subsequently reported:

> ... the battalion charging in successive waves carried all before them, but, I regret to say, suffered severe causalities [*sic*] in doing so. Four officers were killed, 14 wounded, and of other ranks 216 were killed and wounded.[3]

Although the capture and destruction of the magazine fort in the Phoenix Park was to signal the start of the rebellion, some of the Volunteers were late arriving at the park. It seems that they engaged in a game of football as a ploy to get closer to the fort. As soon as the players were in close proximity, they jumped the unsuspecting sentry and gained access. The commander was away but his wife, Mrs Playfair, and her two sons and daughter were allowed time to evacuate before the rebels attempted to blow up the fort. One of the Volunteer officers, Paddy Daly, warned them not to raise the alarm when they were released. The rebels, failing to gain access to the high-explosives store, set off explosives in the adjoining room hoping that this would penetrate the powder-room, but this also failed. They then raided a small arms store, making off with a number of rifles. One of the Playfair boys managed to escape and ran to try and raise the alarm. He was followed by one of the Volunteers on a bicycle, who caught up with him as he banged on the door of a house near Islandbridge Road. As the door opened, the Volunteer shot the seventeen-year-old three times, and he died on the spot. Back in the Phoenix Park, the rebels set fire to the fort before leaving, but the army ordnance department at Islandbridge raised the alarm and the fire brigade lost no time in arriving to extinguish the flames.[4]

At about 12.45 p.m. that day Michael Kent left home to make funeral arrangements for his Aunt Liz. While doing so he was told that the GPO had been attacked and that shots had been fired in Sackville Street. He returned home to find a number of relations gathered there, telling similar stories of a rebellion. A neighbour arrived with the most serious news thus far, saying that some cavalry soldiers had been shot. After dinner Michael ventured out again to try to complete the funeral arrangements. While on his way to Phibsboro he came across a number of barricades manned by Volunteers. A motorcar, which he assumed had been commandeered, whizzed past him carrying Volunteers with guns poised. Michael was immediately struck by the youth of many of the Volunteers and similar to other spectators, he thought it was a 'terrible mad business'. Michael noticed that by 4 p.m. the trams had stopped running and that, with the exception of some cavalry trying to find a safe route back to barracks, the police and military had disappeared off the streets. He watched as the commanding officer of a cavalry regiment gazed anxiously along the Grand Canal. Michael believed that this regiment was returning from an unsuccessful attack on the GPO and was obviously trying to avoid any further encounter with the rebels.[5]

12

Securing the Union

Having left his wife and son, Éamonn Ceannt walked briskly to meet the Fourth Battalion, assembled at Emerald Square, Dolphin's Barn. His mobilisation orders were for 11 a.m. When all the Volunteers had assembled, the tall, lean figure of Ceannt addressed them, saying that an Irish Republic had been declared. He also told them that they were now going into action and that the objective was to occupy the South Dublin Union complex and hold it at all costs. His address was short and at about 11.35 a.m. the Volunteers marched off to take up their positions. Only 120 men of the 700-strong battalion turned out. Ceannt had expected at least 500, but the poor response did not seem to disturb him. Those who did take their place in the ranks were in excellent spirits; many of them had long awaited this day. He split his small force into five groups. The first group consisted of about a dozen cyclists and a number of men on foot, which he would lead himself. They were to enter the South Dublin Union complex via the rear entrance at Rialto. Three parties of twenty Volunteers were to set up outposts: the first at Jameson's Distillery in Marrowbone Lane, commanded by Captain Séamus Murphy; another at Watkin's Brewery in Ardee Street, under Captain Con Colbert; and the third at Roe's Distillery in James's Street where Captain Thomas MacCarthy would be in command. The larger force under Vice-Commandant Brugha would march to the main entrance at James's Street.[1]

The South Dublin Union (now St James's Hospital) was a workhouse complex covering over fifty-two acres. At that time it was the largest outlying group of buildings in the west of the city. The complex consisted of streets, alleys and court-yards, and was studded with hospital buildings consisting of halls, dormitories and wards, and other buildings such as churches and sheds. Several acres of open fields spread south-wards from the main group of buildings at the James's Street entrance. These fields were known as the MacCaffrey Estate, Orchard Fields and the Master's Fields. It was in these fields that most of the Volunteer casualties occurred. The whole complex was surrounded by a high stone wall which gave it the appearance of a small, fortified town. Its southern wall, flanking the Grand Canal, was about half a mile long. During the rebellion there were 3,282 inmates and a number of staff in the complex. Ceannt was faced with an almost im-possible task: how was he going to adequately defend such a large area with his drastically reduced force? Even with a large force the complex would be difficult to defend. Because of this he had to curtail his carefully laid plans – the full im-pact of MacNeill's countermanding orders was now realised.

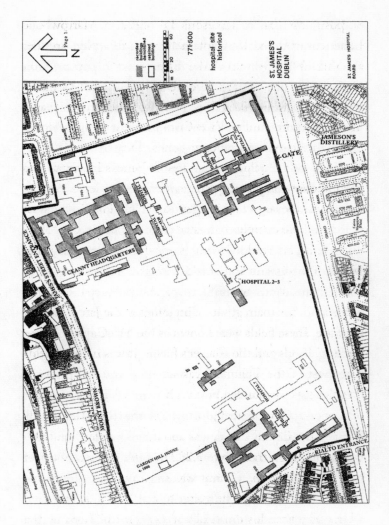

Map of the South Dublin Union. The map, from an original by St James's Teaching Hospital, has been altered to include only those buildings which existed in 1916 (*courtesy of St James's Hospital, Dublin*).

Ceannt's high standing on the military council is apparent from the vital area he was given to command. The South Dublin Union was one of the most important links in the chain of positions held by the Volunteers. Ceannt's strategic position was close to both Richmond and Islandbridge Barracks and could control much of the movement along the quays. It was strategically located near Kingsbridge station, through which British reinforcements from the military camp at the Curragh would be deployed. The complex was also close to the Royal Hospital, Kilmainham, the British military headquarters in Ireland.[2]

Ceannt, followed by his party, proceeded along the banks of the Grand Canal to Rialto Bridge. At noon, they entered the complex through a small door at the corner of Brookfield Road, Rialto. The only opposition they met was the astonished porter, who Ceannt simply pushed aside, grabbing the keys to the complex. The telephone wires were cut immediately, preventing any call for help. Ceannt assigned nine Volunteers under the command of Captain George Irvine to guard the Rialto entrance. They immediately occupied a long narrow building which dominated the entrance. The building was 300 feet long, 26 feet wide and was divided into six dormitories. It was constructed of thin corrugated iron and was used to house the male inmates, who were withdrawn by the staff to dormitory 6, in the safest end of the building. The Volunteers lost no time preparing for action and erected barricades. The walls of the building would not provide much protection from rifle fire, but it was the only building dominating the entrance which could be successfully occupied in a short time. Meanwhile Ceannt had set off across the Union grounds to rendezvous with Cathal Brugha and the rest of his command who were advancing on the James's Street entrance. They quickly covered the half-mile route and both parties arrived at the entrance simultaneously. The Volunteers entered the front courtyard to the distant sounds of a military band. A slight breeze carried the music from the direction of Richmond Barracks. Turning to one of the Volunteers, Ceannt happily remarked, 'They do not know yet.' Almost as he spoke the music suddenly stopped and Ceannt knew that the alarm had just been raised. When all the Volunteers had entered the Union complex, the arch gate was shut and a barricade was erected. A number of Volunteers then occupied the offices above the arch, which ran along most of the short front to the Union building. From this position they could overlook James's Street and they began to fortify their position immediately by erecting more barricades on some of the windows. The Volunteers then tunnelled through each of the internal adjoining walls within the building, allowing them to traverse the entire block without having to leave cover.[3]

Éamonn Ceannt proved himself an excellent military tactician. In preparation for the conflict he split his small force and placed them at strategic points from which he calculated the enemy would advance. He assumed that troops from Richmond and Islandbridge Barracks would march along the southern bank of the River Liffey to reach the city centre. In the event of this happening, MacCarthy's men in Roe's Distillery would engage the enemy. He was also prepared if the enemy chose the parallel inland route along Old Kilmainham and up the slight hill at Mount Brown. He placed an officer and four men at the extreme corner of Mount Brown and Brookfield Road. They were hidden behind a low wall on the Union side of Mount Brown Road which dropped steeply to the pavement on the outside. Closer to the main Union buildings he placed another officer and eight men concealed by thick hedging. The Volunteers in this section were under the command of John Joyce and Lieutenant William O'Brien. If the British military decided not to pass the Union and instead moved along Brookfield Road towards Rialto Bridge, they would come under fire from the Volunteers at Jameson's Distillery. An officer and five men guarded the rear wall of the Union along the Grand Canal, while five Volunteers protected the eastern boundary. Eight men occupied the building known as Hospital 2–3, situated about 250 yards from the Rialto gate. Finally, one Volunteer took up a rather dangerous position, digging into a shallow trench in front of the Rialto gate close to George Irvine's position. Although Ceannt had no more than sixty-five men in total at any time within the Union complex, he still managed to deploy men to all the important positions.[4]

One of Ceannt's officers was Lieutenant William T.

Cosgrave, who later became the first leader of the executive council of the Irish Free State. Upon entering the Union, Lieutenant Cosgrave became concerned about the actual size of the area which they would have to defend. He believed that trying to hold the whole complex was hopeless and mentioned this to Brugha, who asked, 'What do you suggest then?' Lieutenant Cosgrave pointed to the Night Nurses' Home, a solid three-storey building situated on the west side of the main courtyard and which was built at right angles to James's Street. Brugha immediately agreed and summoned Ceannt, who subsequently decided to occupy it as his headquarters. From the back of the building, British military advances could be curtailed in areas such as MacCaffrey's Estate, Mount Brown, Brookfield Road and the Rialto gate. After the building had been secured, most of the windows were smashed and barricaded. Ceannt then stationed a number of marksmen at the top back windows. Most of the inmates, patients and staff were evacuated to safer buildings and Red Cross flags were then displayed on these buildings. The bravery of the hospital staff was apparent, all of whom stayed throughout the fighting to care for the patients and the wounded. The two chaplains, Fr Dillon and Fr Gerhard, were there to minister to those who needed the last rites. Free access for provisions to the hospitals was allowed throughout the week.[5]

13

Attack on the Union

Within about forty minutes of the occupation of the South Dublin Union the British military made their appearance. A column of about 100 soldiers from the Third Royal Irish Regiment began making their way to the city centre. They were under the command of Lieutenant-Colonel R. L. Owen and his adjutant, Captain Roche Kelly. Upon reaching the bottom of Mount Brown, they halted and scanned the streets up ahead. It seems that the Volunteers at the corner of Mount Brown made no effort to conceal themselves behind the low wall. There was an air of uneasiness about the place and the silent empty street offered no encouragement to the soldiers to proceed. One officer, Lieutenant George Malone, was ordered to march forward with twenty men. Five soldiers in advance of the main column were allowed to pass the James's Street entrance. However, when the main column reached this position, they were met by a sudden barrage of heavy fire at almost point-blank range from three Volunteer positions. Three soldiers were shot down immediately and the others took whatever cover was available, some entering the neighbouring houses and buildings. The British company sergeant showed tremendous courage under the heavy fire and managed to get most of his men to safety by battering down the door of a tanyard, which was almost opposite the rebel positions. As the troops rushed in, one of them was shot dead. Lieutenant Malone tried to pull the dead soldier inside and was also shot but managed to reach safety before collapsing. Some of the soldiers returned fire, killing Volunteer John Owens and wounding at least two others. The remainder of the British column at the bottom of Mount Brown opened fire on the rebel positions, covering the retreat of their comrades. When all the survivors had reached safety, the firing temporarily ceased.[1]

The party of British troops at the foot of Mount Brown was split into three groups. One group was sent to take up positions in the Royal Hospital, Kilmainham, less than 300 yards away, as some rebel positions could be dominated from the top of this building. The main party, led by Captain Edward Warmington, Lieutenant Alan Ramsay and Major Milner were sent to attack the rear of the Union complex. The third group was preparing to attack the James's Street entrance. Captain Warmington and Lieutenant Ramsay made their way to the Rialto gate and split into smaller groups. One party crossed the bridge at Rialto and occupied the buildings on the far side of the canal. Some entered buildings opposite the entrance, while the others prepared for an assault on the gate.

On hearing the earlier blasts of gunfire from James's Street, the Volunteers occupying the outposts at the rear entrance knew that within a short time they would be under attack. They did not have long to wait and at 1 p.m. the deathly silence was broken by a ferocious simultaneous military assault on both the front and rear of the Union complex. At the Rialto entrance, fusillade after fusillade was fired into the corrugated building where Irvine's section was stationed. The bullets ripped through both walls. Military fire from across the canal caught the rebels in a deadly crossfire, showering through the gable of the building. One of the Volunteers' best marksmen, seventeen-year-old John Traynor, was killed shortly after hostilities broke out. Irvine went to his aid, but Traynor was mortally wounded. The attack was also supported by machine-gun fire from the roof of the Royal Hospital.[2]

The Rialto gate held, but nearby a small door was forced open and the military poured through. Lieutenant Ramsay, leading the attack, was met with a hail of fire from the rebel positions. Ramsay was shot through the head and, under heavy rebel fire, the military were forced to retreat. A stretcher party was permitted to remove the officer's body. Upon hearing of the death of his fellow officer and friend, Captain Warmington became infuriated and made the fatal mistake of leading a second charge and rushing the rebel positions, and he was also shot dead. With the second commanding officer dead, the military panicked and, under rebel fire, retreated. The stretcher party was again permitted and the body of the second officer was removed and laid down beside his friend.

At the corner of Mount Brown, the Volunteers under Joyce and O'Brien were also under assault. An enormous mass of bullets swept over the Volunteer positions from the front, rear and both flanks. Open fields lay between the Volunteers and the temporary safety of the Union buildings. Although it seemed impossible to survive in the open, they were left with no choice but to run the lethal gauntlet. The only cover the fields offered were slight hollows and ridges. The order to retreat was given and the Volunteers spread out and began a series of short, fast runs for the cover of the hollows, turning to fire as they went. Deadly fire from the roof of the Royal Hospital ripped up the open ground, slowing down the rebel retreat. The rebels were pinned to the ground and those who were not hit had to crawl, unable even to raise their heads. It took Joyce and the surviving Volunteers an hour and a half to reach the cover of one of the hospital buildings, the Women's Hospital.[3]

The attack on the Rialto entrance was proving too costly for the military. More troops had already begun moving up along the canal bank, running just outside the southern wall. About 500 yards along the canal route they reached a large gate. Just as they were forcing an entry to the complex, they came under a hail of rebel fire from Jameson's Distillery on the opposite side of the canal. The troops were caught in the open; some flung themselves to the ground, others tried to scale the ten-foot wall, but were also fired on from inside the Union. One officer who managed to scale the wall was shot through the head as he straddled the wall. Another soldier climbed up behind a telegraph pole for cover but was also hit, his body bouncing off the edge of the canal before he splashed into the water. Eventually the troops forced open the large gate and, although sustaining several casualties, a considerable number of them entered the Union grounds. The rebel fire continued but the onslaught of military firepower forced them to retreat.[4]

Hospital 2–3 lay in the path of the rebel retreat and would provide temporary cover if they could manage to cross the intervening fields. But reaching the hospital proved extremely difficult, the area was being swept with continuous gunfire, and during the retreat three Volunteers were killed: Richard O'Reilly, Brendan Donelan and James Quinn. At the Rialto gate, Irvine's position was becoming desperate and he sent a dispatch to Ceannt requesting instructions. In the return dispatch, Ceannt ordered a withdrawal to some of the main buildings. However, by the time the handwritten reply reached them, the situation had changed, making the orders impractical. A second dispatch was sent but the messenger, when returning with the new orders, found himself completely cut off from his section. Irvine's section was now isolated, but they fought back furiously. The gunfire was so intense that they had to take turns shooting as their rifles were becoming almost too hot to handle. The superior firepower of the British military eventually gained the upper hand and they charged forward, broke into the barricaded building and forced Irvine and his men to surrender.[5]

Crown forces then overran the southern area of the Union, but they still had to cross the open ground to attack rebel positions in Hospital 2–3. From the upper windows of the hospital, the rebels fired furiously into the military ranks. The military managed to reach the hospital wall in a series of short fast runs, dropping for ground cover from time to time. When they broke into the central courtyard at the rear of the hospital they encountered two Volunteers guarding the ground floor. The Volunteers opened fire immediately and rushed for cover in the dormitories, followed closely by the military. The Volunteers ran through the maze of corridors, turning at short intervals to return fire. Upon reaching the front of the building, they dived through a window, both tumbling out onto the lawn amid the shattering glass and flying lead. As they rose one of the rebels turned to fire but took a gunshot in the stomach. He immediately shouted to his companion to run on, saying that he had been hit. The other Volunteer rising from his position ran towards the main group of buildings and, as he got there, the military suddenly appeared from the side of the hospital. He opened fire on them while running, forcing them to retreat into one of the buildings. He succeeded in reaching one of the main buildings and escaped around a corner, almost running into Commandant Ceannt who was attending a wounded Volunteer shot during a reconnaissance mission. They tried to return to Ceannt's headquarters but were cut off by the sudden rush of military coming through the canal gate. They decided not to move the wounded man until they located a safe exit. Both men then retreated down a cul-de-sac between two hospital buildings, at the end of which was a large wooden gate. Ceannt tried in vain to force the gate open but they were trapped at the end of the alley. They prepared for a last stand. Ceannt checked his pistol, preparing to make it a costly attack for the military, but the expected attack never came. An inmate who was watching from the window of a nearby building came to their aid. He managed to secure a ladder and lowered it to the narrow street below. The rebel leader ordered his companion to mount the ladder first, while he kept his weapon trained on the entrance to the alley, still expecting the military to appear at any moment. After the Volunteer had reached safety, he turned and covered Ceannt as he followed. Ceannt immediately instructed the matron of the hospital to bring the wounded Volunteer to safety. However, they still had to run the gauntlet to reach the headquarters. Having consulted his map, Ceannt decided the route of escape was through the rear of the hospital. Their retreat was covered by some remaining Volunteer positions.[6]

Ceannt must have wondered why the military had not followed through with the attack. One possible reason was that the soldiers had turned their attention to the six rebels who were occupying the upper floor of Hospital 2–3. These rebels were forced back to the west wing of the hospital where a young nurse, Margaret Keogh, was on duty. There was a temporary lull in the firing, which led Nurse Keogh to believe that the military assault on the building was over. Turning to a companion she said, 'Thank God there will be no bloodshed here.' Suddenly the silence was broken by the thunder of gunshots from downstairs. Nurse Keogh, fearful for the safety of the patients, panicked and ran down the stairs. The military had taken up positions in a long corridor to the left at the bottom of the stairwell. When Nurse Keogh appeared in the opening, the soldiers opened fire, killing her instantly. Her friend who had followed screamed but the commanding officer shouted to her, 'Are there any Sinn Féiners upstairs?' She begged the soldiers to remove the dead body of her friend from the floor, which they did, and placed it on a table. At that moment the young Volunteer who had been shot in the stomach was carried into the hospital by one of the inmates. It seems that the look on the young man's face told those present that he did not have very long to live.

A large military force now pressed forward with their search of the hospital. They proceeded to the top floor and, using a pass-key, gained access to one of the wings. Before entering the room, they called out to the rebels to surrender. When they didn't receive a reply the military attacked. The fighting took place at very close quarters and developed into a fierce hand-to-hand struggle before the Volunteers were eventually forced to surrender.[7]

By mid-afternoon there were heavy losses on both sides, and the military launched a direct assault on the Women's Hospital. This hospital was occupied by a number of Volunteers, including Section Commander Joyce, who had survived the retreat from Mount Brown. Joyce and his men waited in deathly silence at the intersection of two wards on one of the upper floors. When the military appeared the Volunteers opened fire. The air was suddenly filled with the sound of gunfire, the smell of gunpowder and the screams of women who had not been evacuated. Joyce and his men were determined not to surrender and scrambled back to one of the wards, slamming the door behind them. The military fired through the door and then ordered them to surrender on the count of five. Back on their feet, Joyce and his comrades ran towards the opposite end of the ward. They shot the lock off the door, kicked it open and ran through to the next ward. The military followed in hot pursuit, firing as they went. Nevertheless, all the rebels eventually managed to break free of their pursuers and reached the safety of Ceannt's headquarters, thus ending hostilities for that day.[8]

When the fighting ceased, those who were not on watch had their first meal of the day – corned beef and tea. While they were eating, Ceannt informed them that the Rising was going well in the city. This announcement lifted their spirits and in thanksgiving they knelt and recited the rosary. It seems that this was the procedure at the South Dublin Union every night throughout the rebellion. Although the Volunteers had been forced back to the main buildings, they had managed to achieve all that the IRB military council could have hoped for with such small numbers. Lieutenant Cosgrave's stepbrother, Goban Burke, had been shot dead at headquarters that day and the body of another Volunteer, William MacDowell, lay in a field close by. Ceannt offered a temporary truce to allow time to remove the dead and wounded, but this was refused by the military. One of the Volunteers, James Coughlan, later said that Ceannt displayed plenty of initiative and led by example throughout the battle. He was obviously very impressed by his commander as he went on to say that Ceannt seemed to tower above all the other officers and that some of the men believed his courage and leadership skills were exemplary. He also said that Ceannt should have delegated more and believed that if anything had happened to him, they would have been finished that first day.[9]

Prior to resting himself, Ceannt paid a visit to the Volunteers stationed at the James's Street entrance and asked if they had enough supplies. They replied that they had bread, but could do with some meat. Ceannt invited one of them to return to headquarters with him, where he gave him a supply of cooked ham to take back to the others. Later, a dispatch rider, Miss Doherty, arrived with word from Pearse, after which Ceannt informed his men that all of Ireland was now in revolt. He told them that on the front lines of the Great War, German troops were holding up posters from the safety of their trenches informing Irish regiments of the rebellion in Ireland. He went on to say that British ships were being attacked in the Irish Sea. Whether this was wishful thinking on Ceannt's part or false information he had received in the dispatch from Pearse is unclear, as the dispatch has never been located. Nevertheless, it had been a hard-won day for the Volunteers, who held their positions. The following quote captures the episode:

> … denied a respite, Ceannt's forces continued to defend the South Dublin Union with stubborn gallantry. All that hard day – that long and brilliant-sunlit, death-hunting day – hunger and thirst had waxed among them … a nerve-racking, heart-stopping battle of unexpected death, with rarely a let-up. A sense of purpose, a flame of patriotism, still flickered strongly.[10]

14

Calm before the Storm

Military operations for the remainder of the week were chiefly confined to the group of buildings near the James's Street entrance. On Tuesday morning Volunteer Frank Burke, who had survived the Mount Brown retreat the previous day, gave the wake-up call to the Volunteers, warning them to be careful of sniper fire – ironically, moments later a sniper's bullet killed him. His body was temporarily buried along with other Volunteer casualties in the Master's Field. Ceannt wrote a card and placed it over the remains: 'Here a hero died for Ireland. May the Lord have mercy on his noble soul.' Later that morning, the Volunteers displayed a national flag from one of the upper windows of the Irish headquarters. Although no material was available, they had improvised by taking a window blind and painting an Irish harp on it. As the flag was being raised, the Volunteers stood to attention and sang 'A Nation Once Again'. This action certainly antagonised the British military as they immediately sprayed heavy fire at the Irish positions from the roof of the Royal Hospital. The military also took action from their hard-won positions within the Union, while their snipers fired almost incessantly throughout the day.

At about 9 p.m. Ceannt established contact with the outposts, only to learn that the Volunteers at Roe's Distillery had abandoned their position and that some of them had joined the garrison at Jameson's Distillery. Con Colbert and his command in Watkin's Brewery had also united forces with Séamus Murphy in Jameson's Distillery, increasing the strength of this section even further. There were also seven members of Fianna Éireann, two Volunteers from another unit and one member of the Citizen Army under Murphy's command. Twenty-three members of Cumann na mBan cooked hot meals for the Volunteers there and attended to the wounded.

The British occupied most of the Union complex but the makeshift republican flag still hung proudly from Ceannt's headquarters. Volunteer ammunition was very meagre, with less than 3,000 rounds remaining to defend the Union. Even at that they were lucky, as at one stage during the week the military had unknowingly occupied a room where some of the rebel ammunition was stored. That same day two civilians were killed during hostilities, a local woman and a visitor from Belfast. Meanwhile in the city, Francis Sheehy-Skeffington, writer and pacifist, went around the streets of Dublin trying to stop people from looting. While engaged in this activity he was arrested by Captain Bowen-Colthurst, whom he had witnessed killing an unarmed boy for breaking curfew. The following morning, along with two journalists, Thomas Dickson and Patrick McIntyre, Sheehy-Skeffington was executed on Captain Bowen-Colthurst's orders.[1]

Éamonn's brother Michael remembered that as the day progressed there were rumours of a large force of German troops landing in Ireland and advancing from Kildare or Limerick. He also heard that Cork, Galway and Dundalk were all ablaze with rebellion. Some of the rebels had also heard these rumours and believed that it was only a matter of time before the rebels, supported by the Germans, reached Dublin. Michael also heard that German submarines had attacked and sunk several troopships making their way from England. That evening the Ceannt family gathered together at Michael's house. At about 7 p.m. they heard 'a tremendous rattle of machine-gun fire'. Both Michael and Richard felt an overwhelming sense of foreboding and imagined Ceannt lying 'stark and stiff in death somewhere'. Michael was very anxious about Áine and Rónán as he had no idea of their whereabouts. The only clue as to where Ceannt was located came when Nell arrived and recounted her experiences from the previous day.

Meanwhile, back at his Union headquarters, Ceannt had gathered his men together again to recite the rosary, after which he told them that he was proud of them and thanked God for giving him the 'great pleasure of leading them'. He also told them that he believed that a major British assault on their position was imminent. On

Wednesday, there was a lull in the fighting and it seemed as though the military had completely withdrawn. The rebels were able to walk freely around the inner courtyard of the Nurses' Home. But it was merely the calm before the storm.[2]

Sir Francis Vane had now taken command of the British troops in the South Dublin Union area. On Easter Monday Sir Francis had been in Bray having lunch with a fellow officer when news came that the principal buildings in Dublin city were in rebel hands. Both men made the dangerous journey back to Portobello (now Cathal Brugha) Barracks, also hearing wild rumours that huge rebel armies assisted by German troops were marching towards Dublin. By Wednesday several British battalions, including the Sherwood Foresters, were arriving from England. More British troops arrived from the Curragh, Belfast, Athlone and Templemore, and RIC personnel were also being called into Dublin. The royal navy steamer, HMS *Helga*, made its way as far as possible up the River Liffey and proceeded to shell Liberty Hall in the mistaken belief that members of the Irish Citizen Army were still inside.

Back at Union headquarters, Martin Ennis, an employee of the Union, gave Ceannt important information regarding the strength of the British. He asked Ceannt if he could join with the rebel forces but Ceannt refused, saying that he was more valuable outside the wall where he could gather and relay information. Ceannt then made arrangements to try and meet with him on a daily basis. After dark, Ceannt left the safety of his headquarters and scaled the Union wall, obviously to meet with his informant. He returned about twenty minutes later with the news that Dublin was on its own and they could expect no support from the rest of the country. He also commented that he was delighted that they were being recognised as soldiers, as the hostilities were being referred to as a rebellion.[3]

Áine had no idea of her husband's situation. Mrs Brugha decided to go out for a walk that night accompanied by her sister and a friend who was also being given shelter at the Brugha home. Áine felt that it was dangerous to venture out in any part of Dublin city at this time, particularly if you were connected in any way with the rebellion. She also felt that Mrs Brugha was taking an even greater risk as she was expecting a baby. She remained behind with her mother and Rónán. Shortly after they had left the house, there was a sudden loud and continuous knocking on the door. Áine knew she would have to answer. As she cautiously opened the door, it was immediately forced open and all three women practically fell into the hall, clearly distressed and shaken. They said they had been challenged by the military a short distance away but instead of halting they had panicked and run back to the house.[4]

Meanwhile, Michael Kent had procured a good supply of potatoes, flour, bacon and tinned foods, though they had run out of coal on Monday and the gas supply had also been cut. They were now cutting up any old timber for firewood. As the evening wore on the family gathered in the front parlour and watched the volumes of smoke rise over the city. In the distance the sound of gunfire broke the silence of the deserted street. Michael's routine for the week was to take his daughter, Joan, to visit Nell to hear if there was any news of Ceannt. Martial law had been declared on Tuesday 25 April which meant that the citizens of Dublin had to be in their homes by 7.30 p.m., but it seems that an extension to 8.30 p.m. was given. Michael later recorded that by this time the sound of warfare was gathering momentum as the thud of heavy artillery was getting closer. He recorded that some Volunteers actually went home at night and returned in the morning to continue the fight. As each day passed, the scramble for provisions was becoming more urgent. They knew that if the fighting continued, supplies would soon be exhausted.[5]

Portrait of Éamonn Ceannt by P. H. Marrinan in Ceannt Barracks,
Curragh Military Barracks, County Kildare
(*courtesy of Ceannt Barracks*).

Old Royal Irish Constabulary Barracks, Ballymoe, County Galway: the birthplace of Éamonn Ceannt (*author's collection*).

The Ceannt family, *c.* 1903. In the back row, second from left are Michael, Richard and Éamonn. Their father, James, is seated in the middle of the front row (*courtesy of the Gallagher collection*).

Éamonn
Ceannt
(*from the Furey
collection*).

A-Company of
the Fourth
Battalion of
Irish
Volunteers,
September
1915 (*courtesy
of the Allen
Library*).

Ceannt in Irish Volunteer uniform (*courtesy of the Allen Library*).

Áine Ceannt with her son, Rónán (*courtesy of the Allen Library*).

The Ceannt family home, 2 Dolphin's Terrace. In 1926 the numbering changed and the house and street became 201 South Circular Road. In 1960 it changed again and is now 283 South Circular Road (*author's collection*).

Éamon de Valera in British custody at Richmond Barracks, 8 May 1916 (*courtesy of Kilmainham Gaol Museum*).

Edward Daly (*from the Furey collection*).

Countess Markievicz (*photo by Lafayette/printed by Coleman's; from the Furey collection*).

Soldiers holding a Dublin street against the rebels
(*courtesy of the Galway County Library collection*).

The Night Nurses' Home, South Dublin Union, Ceannt's
headquarters during the Rising (*courtesy of Professor Davis Coakley*).

Open ground near Hospital 1 and 2, South Dublin Union
(*courtesy of Professor Davis Coakley*).

James's Street entrance of the South Dublin Union
(*courtesy of Professor Davis Coakley*).

View of Hospital 1, South Dublin Union (St James's Hospital) (*author's collection*).

View of the Royal Hospital, Kilmainham, from the rear of Ceannt's headquarters. The houses in the foreground would not have existed in 1916, so there would have been a much clearer view between the two buildings (*author's collection*).

Sir Francis Vane
(*courtesy of Professor Davis Coakley*).

Irish Rebellion – May 1916.
Soldiers bivouacking opposite Liberty Hall,
the Rebel Headquarters in Dublin.

Soldiers bivouacking opposite Liberty Hall
(*courtesy of the Galway County Library collection*).

Images of Sackville Street (*courtesy of the Galway County Library collection*):
Top: The street in flames.
Bottom: The street part-barricaded with motorcars.

Images of Sackville Street (*courtesy of the Galway County Library collection*):
Top: The street in ruins.
Bottom: East side of the street from O'Connell Bridge.

Irish Rebellion - May 1916.

A group of officers with the captured rebel flag
(*courtesy of the Galway County Library collection*).

The O'Rahilly (*photo by Lafayette/printed by Coleman's*).

Cathal Brugha (*courtesy of Mercier Archives*).

Thomas Clarke (*photo by Keogh Bros/printed by Coleman's*).

Seán Heuston (*photo by Keogh Bros/ printed by Powell Press; from the Furey collection*).

Joseph Plunkett (*printed by Powell Press; from the Furey collection*).

Major John MacBride (*printed by Coleman's; from the Furey collection*).

William Pearse (*photo by Keogh Bros/printed by Coleman's*).

Patrick Pearse (*photo by Lafayette/ printed by Coleman's*).

Michael Mallin (*photo by Keogh Bros/printed by Powell Press; from the Furey collection*).

Thomas Kent (*from the Furey collection*).

Seán Mac Diarmada (*photo by Keogh Bros/printed by Coleman's*).

Thomas MacDonagh (*photo by Keogh Bros/printed by Coleman's*).

James Connolly (*photo by Lafayette/printed by Coleman's; from the Furey collection*).

Kilmainham Gaol (*author's collection*).

Sinn Féin Ard-Fheis, 23 May 1922.
Front row, from left: Áine Ceannt, Éamonn Duggan, Kathleen Lynn,
Arthur Griffith, Éamon de Valera, Michael Collins, Harry Boland
and Hannah Sheehy-Skeffington (*courtesy of the Allen Library*).

15

Final Assault

On Thursday, the British launched a major attack on
Ceannt's headquarters. The fighting began when rifle fire
from the Nurses' Home and Jameson's Distillery held
up British troops being deployed to the Royal Hospital,
Kilmainham. The South Dublin Union would have to be
taken before the large military column could pass the rebel
positions. One of the British commanding officers was
Lieutenant-Colonel W. C. Oates, whose son, Captain John
Oates, was involved in the attack on the Irish headquarters.
The other commanding officer was Captain Mickey
Martyn. The officers sent for assistance to Portobello
Barracks and Sir Francis Vane immediately responded by
leading an additional fifty troops into the attack. Another
British soldier involved in the assault was Monk Gibbon,
who later became a well-known poet and novelist.

By about 3 p.m. the rebel positions had come under
heavy fire from the large body of troops now employed in
the offensive. Troops under Sir Francis Vane and Captain
Martyn advanced in a fan-like sweeping formation across

the open ground towards the rebel stronghold as Captain John Oates and his party provided covering fire from the Rialto entrance. The troops attacked in short rushes, advancing, then dropping to return fire and again rushing forward. The military covering fire was so intense and sustained that it became almost impossible for the rebels to move within the building. The gunfire seemed to be coming from all directions and was ripping through the timber, plaster, walls and ceilings. Although it proved very difficult to return fire, the Volunteers did manage to inflict a number of casualties.

Once Vane and his party had reached the main Union buildings, Captain Oates, accompanied by one of his men, decided to follow. They managed to reach Martyn's platoon only to find that Martyn had already gone on ahead to try to find access to the Nurses' Home. As they were checking on Martyn's whereabouts, rebel fire forced them to take cover in a nearby left-flanking building, where they located Captain Martyn. In this exchange of fire a rebel bullet very narrowly missed Sir Francis Vane's head, striking a wall and showering fragments all over him.[1]

Oates again provided covering fire while Martyn and his platoon made a dash for a series of low buildings on the left flank of the Nurses' Home. Once he had gained his objective, Martyn began making his way through the building towards the rebel position. However, his advance came to an abrupt end when he reached a solid wall. He immediately sent men to Oates and to request tools for knocking a hole in the wall. Troops were then sent to attack the rebels' right flank, some occupying a bakehouse just beyond their target. Although the rebel fire was heavy, it was generally inaccurate. The military lost only one soldier and another was severely wounded. Two soldiers remained in the bakehouse to give covering fire. This attack failed as Ceannt and a number of others, who had gained access to this area by tunnelling through interior walls, opened fire from inside the building.

With the attack repulsed, it was up to Oates and Martyn to force an entry through the wall. The rebels had already erected a huge barricade, about eight feet high, behind the main entrance. A number of rebels took up positions behind the barricade and also on the stairs and landing behind. Captain Martyn and a Sergeant Walker began digging their way through the wall. Once the wall was breached, Martyn, Walker and some military personnel crossed the room towards the lobby, only to be confronted by rapid fire from over the rebel barricade, just inside the entrance. A burst of gunfire from the barricade left three soldiers dead in the lobby. However, the surviving military dived beneath the barricade for cover. One of them managed to lob a bomb over the barricade which exploded seconds later, wounding Cathal Brugha. Oates, who had already followed Martyn into the Nurses' Home, began firing rapidly at the barricade and beyond, hitting Brugha again.

According to Lieutenant Cosgrave, a definite order to

retreat was given after the military had broken into the rebel headquarters. He said that he received this order from Captain Douglas fFrench Mullen, who he believed received it from Commandant Brugha. There were now only twenty-seven men in the Nurses' Home and it seems that just as the blast of gunfire was heard coming from the lobby, Ceannt was on his way to recall the Volunteers who were still occupying the buildings at James's Street. It was suggested later that it was this action combined with the gun-battle at the barricade which caused Brugha to order the retreat.[2]

Although badly wounded, Brugha managed to drag himself through a passageway and into a small kitchen where he turned and faced the direction of the barricade. Loading his weapon, he prepared to meet whatever challenge came before him. This is how Section Commander Joyce found Brugha while making his way to one of the outside dormitories where the other rebels had regrouped. Joyce immediately went to his aid but Brugha simply gave him his watch and told him to give it to his wife, if he got out alive. He then asked for a drink of water, after which he ordered Joyce to join the other Volunteers, advising him to tell Ceannt that he would hold out as long as possible. Joyce then carefully made his way to the courtyard at the rear of the building and, crossing the courtyard, entered the dormitory to join the other rebels.

At this stage Ceannt was obviously feeling the pressure and was arguing with Cosgrave, who was telling him that the British had not breached the barricade and that they should return to their posts. Ceannt was still not convinced and showed little interest even when Joyce reported that Brugha was badly wounded and was manning the barricade alone. Ceannt then told his men they had all put up a good fight, that there was no question of surrender and that they would fight to the last man. Shortly afterwards, the sound of Brugha singing 'God Save Ireland' could be heard. Going outside to the courtyard, they found him propped up against the wall of the rear doorway. From his position he had his gun trained on the barricade and between bursts of fire he was singing and calling on the military to attack. His courage in the face of almost certain death inspired Ceannt and the others. Ceannt approached Brugha and knelt down on one knee putting his arms around him. They spoke in Irish for about a minute. Tears were streaming down Ceannt's face when he stood up to resume command. He immediately ordered his men back to their posts, where they went with renewed vigour.[3]

The rebels were determined not to be taken and once again their guns blazed away, holding back the military. Captain Martyn made his way back to the main force to report the situation while Captain Oates remained behind and, determined to stay alive, began throwing bombs into the lobby every two to three minutes. Prior to the bombs being used, Sir Francis Vane was unsure if there were any British troops still in the building. He called out to those inside but the only reply was 'Go to Hell'. Shortly afterwards, Martyn returned with orders to withdraw. It was about 9.30 p.m. when the military began making their way back through the Union grounds towards Rialto, unknowingly leaving one of their men behind in the bakehouse. At one point Ceannt had a young British soldier in his sights, but the soldier turned to retreat under a Red Cross flag and so Ceannt withheld fire. Sir Francis Vane's assault on rebel headquarters was witnessed by Brigadier-General E. W. S. Maconchy, who recommended that he should be 'mentioned in dispatches'. In later life, Sir Francis and William Cosgrave became friends.

As darkness fell over the Union, it returned to comparative quietness. Away towards the city centre the night sky had turned bright crimson as a result of the raging fires of rebellion.[4]

16

The Galway Rebellion

Towards the end of holy week, Liam Mellows had returned to County Galway to set about finalising the rebellion plans. During that week the Volunteer officers in Galway (including Éamonn Corbett, Joseph Howley, Pádraic Fahy, Matthew Neilan and their commanding officer, Larry Lardner) called a meeting to discuss the situation. It was decided that Lardner would travel to Dublin on Holy Thursday to clarify instructions for the rebellion. Unfortunately, when he arrived in Dublin, he could not locate Pearse or MacNeill, but he did meet with Bulmer Hobson, who instructed him not to obey any orders unless Eoin MacNeill signed them. Lardner returned to Galway more confused than when he had left. Meanwhile Éamonn Ceannt had already sent him a dispatch ordering the rebellion to go ahead as scheduled. It was Frank Fahy's wife who brought the signed orders for Lardner but she was unable to locate him. Eventually she met and gave the dispatch to Volunteer Éamonn Corbett, who assured her that he would give it to Lardner. The dispatch read:

'Collect the Premiums, 7 p.m. Sunday – P. H. Pearse.' This was the agreed code for the rebellion, but the following day Lardner also received MacNeill's orders suspending manoeuvres. An emergency meeting was held at the home of the prominent nationalist George Nicholas in Galway city. It was decided to go ahead and prepare for action while another messenger went to Dublin but this plan also proved unsuccessful. As director of communications, Ceannt had done all within his power to ensure a countrywide rebellion, but even in Dublin the IRB was struggling to overrule MacNeill's orders. His statement to the press cancelling manoeuvres had killed off any hope of a simultaneous rebellion throughout Ireland.[1]

On Sunday, Liam Mellows learned of MacNeill's orders and reluctantly prepared to cancel the rebellion. At about 1 p.m. on Easter Monday, the Athenry Battalion of Volunteers received the following dispatch from Dublin: 'We are out from twelve o'clock today. Issue your orders without delay. – P.H.P.' It was delivered to Lardner's house by a Miss Browne, the future wife of Seán MacEntee (who became a founder member of Fianna Fáil). Because of all the contradicting dispatches, there was still some doubt and uncertainty among the men of the west, but later that afternoon the Dublin train brought news of the rebellion. Dispatches were immediately issued to the South Galway Volunteers, which resulted in about 500 badly-armed men joining the rebellion. The RIC in Oranmore evacuated their barracks and Volunteers under the command of

Captain Joseph Howley began placing explosives under the bridge leading into the town. But British troops and police reinforcements arrived from Galway city, forcing a rebel withdrawal. Mellows provided covering fire for his men during the retreat, resulting in several policemen being wounded. According to the Galway correspondent for the *Daily Mail*, the rebel army actually came within three miles of the city on the Tuesday, but was forced to retreat as a result of shellfire from naval gunships in Galway Bay.[2]

Larry Lardner and his company had occupied the agricultural college and model farm just outside Athenry and the Volunteers retreating from Oranmore joined his garrison. In the town of Athenry the police remained virtual prisoners in their own barracks. Lardner's force had increased to about 500 men, representing many areas including Oranmore, Maree, Clarenbridge, Craughwell, Castlegar, Claregalway, Cregmore and Derrydonnell. Their munitions consisted of 25 rifles, 350 shotguns and an assortment of small arms. Although most of the country was against the rebellion, this does not seem to have been the case in the rebel-held areas of County Galway. The local population in these areas seems to have welcomed the rebellion. The absence of landlords, land agents and armed police gave them their first glimpse of a free society. Farmers' daughters supplied the Volunteers with freshly-baked bread which was washed down with milk. Many Volunteers were made welcome and given 'excellent meals' in the farmhouses.[3]

It seems that Mellows had planned to unite his forces and then move south towards the River Shannon, raising the country into action as he went. On Wednesday morning a force of RIC was attacked at Carnmore, which resulted in the death of one Constable P. Whelan and the wounding of an inspector. That evening, the Volunteers at Athenry moved to Moyode Castle, the unoccupied home of the Persse family and Mellows made it his headquarters. By now British troops and marines had landed at Galway docks and were preparing for action. Several Volunteer officers in Galway city, among them George Nicholas, were arrested and taken on board one of the warships. At Moyode, animals were slaughtered as required and the women of Cumann na mBan acted as cooks and nurses. In the distance, the sound of naval artillery fire could be heard coming from the direction of Galway Bay. On Thursday evening the Volunteers held a meeting and it was decided to disband the unarmed men, thus reducing the force to about 400.

Although he had not seen any real action, Mellows was determined to fight to the last man if necessary. However, the majority of his officers were in favour of disbanding. Police from the northern counties were now arriving in County Galway and were arresting some of the Volunteers who were making their way home. On Friday evening the remainder of the Volunteers, about 150, moved southwards until they reached a large unoccupied mansion at Limepark and set up another headquarters. A local priest, Fr Thomas

Fahy, brought news that British troops were on the move from Athlone and Ballinasloe and he also told them that the rebellion in Dublin was collapsing. Having heard this news, Mellows reluctantly followed Fr Fahy's advice and the Volunteers were disbanded.[4]

Three Volunteers, Frank Hynes, Peadar Howley and Ailbhe Ó Monncháin, chose to remain with Mellows and became fugitives with him. Having taken shelter in a number of locations in the mountains and woods, they eventually found a safe refuge at Tulla, just south of Kinvara. Mellows remained there for four months, during which time he visited Kinvara where he took shelter in the Convent of Mercy of St Joseph. The authorities were obviously informed of this because they conducted a search of the convent. When Fr Thomas Burke, parish priest of Kinvara, was informed of the search, he was outraged and wrote a letter of protest to General Sir John Maxwell. In his reply, Maxwell stated that the local police sergeant had been informed by means of an anonymous letter that Mellows was hiding in the convent. He went on to say that the sergeant felt it was his duty to capture Mellows and that, as far as he was concerned, the search was 'carried out with perfect decorum'. Eventually Mellows enlisted the help of some members of the clergy and this time made his escape disguised as a nun. Having evaded capture for a number of months, Mellows made his way to Liverpool and from there managed to secure passage on board a steamer bound for America.[5]

17

Surrender

Thursday's attack was the last serious assault on Ceannt's position, and from then until the surrender on Sunday there was only sporadic gunfire around the Union grounds. Although there were only twenty-seven Volunteers in the main building and sixteen at the James's Street entrance during the attack, the military believed that the numbers were much higher. After the successful defence of his headquarters, Ceannt deliberated what the outcome would have been had all the Volunteers gone into action.

The battle for the South Dublin Union took place in extraordinary circumstances and was unparalleled in the other areas of the rebellion. In the labyrinth of intersecting passages no one knew from where the fatal shot might be fired and at which moment their life would end. Danger lurked everywhere and at times the Volunteers and military had occupied the same buildings. Captain Martyn later stated:

I found a bullet in Dublin every bit as dangerous as a bullet in No Man's Land. In some ways the fighting in Dublin was worse. In France you generally had an idea where the enemy was and where the bullets were going to come from. In Dublin you never knew when or from where you were going to be hit.[1]

On Friday morning, Ceannt allowed a party of Union officials and inmates freedom of movement to remove the military personnel who had been killed the previous day. The soldier still concealed in the bakehouse took his chance and made a daring and sensational escape. He watched as the body of a fallen comrade was placed in a coffin. While the coffin was being placed in the hearse, the soldier left his place of security and quickly entered an empty coffin nearby. Obviously the part-time undertakers did not notice the live cargo and placed the lid on the coffin. The coffins were removed to a mortuary at Rialto where the soldier made his reappearance, rising from the coffin to the bewilderment of all those present.

By this time, the sound of heavy artillery seemed to be getting closer and Ceannt gathered his men together to issue instructions should artillery be used against their headquarters. Leading them to the rear of the building he pointed to the fields where they would dig trenches, indicating that he did not expect to surrender.[2]

Back at Fitzwilliam Terrace, Áine escaped detection during a military raid that morning. The military entered the house, only to find that it was occupied by women and children. The soldiers asked why there were no men present and Mrs Brugha informed the commanding officer that her husband's work took him around the country and that he had been held up and was unable to return to Dublin because of the rebellion. They obviously did not recognise Áine and left the house without questioning her. Fr Kingston, who was Mrs Brugha's brother, arrived that evening with news that Brugha had been wounded but reassured them that he was not in any danger.[3]

At Sackville Street the GPO had been reduced to a smoky ruin under the heavy barrage of fire from the British artillery. By 8 p.m. incendiary shells had set the top of the building ablaze. Pearse was forced to evacuate his position and withdrew to buildings in Moore Street. During the evacuation, The O'Rahilly, along with many others, was killed by a blast of machine-gun fire. That evening a newspaper reporter, John O'Leary, watched the destruction of the GPO from across the River Liffey:

> The fire grows and grows, seems to bubble as heaps of glowing debris crash over the granite walls and through the flame-heated windows. High above the doomed building, the Republican flag flutters in the stifling atmosphere of smoke. Leaping flames lick and kiss the pole on which it hangs. With my field glasses I can see the letters IRISH REPUBLIC scorch to a deep brown. Now and then the flag is buried as thousands of fragments of burning paper belch up as if it were from a volcano. At 9 p.m. the G.P.O. is in ruins, its granite walls look like the bones of a skeleton skull.[4]

On Saturday morning, Pearse, Clarke, Mac Diarmada, Plunkett and a badly-wounded Connolly held a meeting in 16 Moore Street. Having discussed the situation, it was decided to try and negotiate surrender terms with the British commander, Brigadier-General Lowe. It seems that Pearse decided to surrender having witnessed the deaths of three civilians killed by military fire. The killings so shocked Pearse that he abandoned the idea of carrying the fight into the streets as originally planned. At 12.45 p.m. the flag of surrender was held out in bullet-swept Moore Street. When the guns fell silent, Nurse Elizabeth O'Farrell stepped into the street and began walking towards the military positions. Upon arrival at the barricade, she informed the military that Commandant Pearse wished to discuss surrender terms with General Lowe. When General Lowe was contacted, his reply was simple: he would only accept an unconditional surrender. Nurse O'Farrell then returned to the rebel headquarters with Lowe's demand and, after another meeting of the war council, it was decided to surrender on Lowe's terms. At almost 2.30 p.m. the commanding figure of Pearse stepped into the street and marched towards the British barricade. General Lowe accepted his surrender and Pearse then presented his sword and revolver to a staff officer, Major de Courcy Wheeler. The rebellion was officially over but the question now was how to force Ceannt and the others to surrender. The order to surrender was signed and sent to the various outposts:

In order to prevent the further slaughter of Dublin citizens, and in the hope of saving the lives of our followers now surrounded and hopelessly outnumbered, the members of the Provisional Government present at Headquarters have agreed to an unconditional surrender, and the Commandants of the various districts in the City and Country will order their commands to lay down arms.

P. H. Pearse

29th April, 3.45 p.m., 1916.

I agree to those conditions for the men only under my own command in the Moore Street District and for the men in the St Stephen's Green command.

James Connolly
April 29/16.[5]

Having surrendered, the Volunteers assembled at the back of Moore Street and marched into Parnell Street, where under the shadow of the Parnell monument they piled their arms. The prisoners were generally treated with respect by the British military but there were, of course, a few exceptions. One in particular was a bad-tempered Irishman in the British army, Captain Lea Wilson, who continually hurled abuse and insults at the Volunteer leaders. It seems that this man later caused problems for the IRA and Michael Collins had him shot dead during the War of Independence.[6]

By now the women at Fitzwilliam Terrace were becoming more and more concerned about their loved ones.

Áine and Mrs Brugha decided to leave the house on Saturday and began to make their way to Rathmines hoping to hear news of the rebels. Along the way they heard some shooting and could see that fires were still burning in the city. Having been informed of a ceasefire they returned to Fitzwilliam Terrace. The following morning, 30 April, Áine attended mass at Rathgar church, where she met Mrs Con Murphy. It was then that Áine learned that a Proclamation declaring an Irish Republic had been issued just prior to the rebellion and that Ceannt had signed the document. This was the first time that Áine had heard of the Proclamation.[7]

On Sunday morning, Nurse O'Farrell brought the surrender orders to Thomas MacDonagh in Jacob's Biscuit Factory. At first MacDonagh refused to accept the orders, but later agreed to meet with two Capuchin priests, Fr Augustine and Fr Aloysius, who also handed him the surrender orders. He said that he would only discuss terms with Brigadier-General Lowe and a short time later a meeting took place between the two men. The result was a temporary ceasefire to allow MacDonagh, accompanied by the two priests, to go to the South Dublin Union and discuss the terms with Éamonn Ceannt. From their positions within the Union the rebels observed two figures appear at the end of James's Street. Soon the figures began to walk towards the Union under the protection of a white flag. As they came closer, word was relayed back to headquarters that one of the men approaching was Thomas MacDonagh and the other was a priest. Ceannt was also against the surrender at first, but considering that Pearse and Connolly had signed the orders he decided to obey. He had had a desire to carry the fight into the streets in the hope that the country would eventually join them in rebellion.

After MacDonagh left, Ceannt called all of his men together and informed them of the unconditional surrender by Pearse and Connolly. He asked them if they wished to express their views on the surrender and some did voice some concerns. They then asked him what his own views on the situation were, to which he replied that, considering Thomas Clarke had surrendered, there was no shame in the South Dublin Union men surrendering. He informed them that heavy artillery and incendiary shells had been used in the city and because of the growing civilian death toll, it had been decided to surrender, thus preventing greater loss of life. Ceannt went on to say that the leaders of the rebellion would receive a 'single journey' while the Volunteers would receive a 'double journey'. If the Volunteers decided to continue the fight then he was prepared to continue to lead the battalion. Having decided on surrender, he ordered that no one should attempt to escape or desert his post. He then told them to collect their weapons and to eat whatever rations they had left and to assemble at the Union entrance within half an hour.[8]

As Ceannt assembled the Volunteers to march out of the Union complex, Sir Francis Vane expressed his amazement that there were only forty men occupying the building. Ceannt simply replied, 'No, Forty-two.' At first, Vane doubted that such a small number of men could have held out against Thursday's attack and suspected that some had already made an escape. However, upon speaking with Ceannt, he accepted his word that this was his complete command. A Red Cross ambulance arrived to take away the wounded while Ceannt led his men out of the Union. Cathal Brugha was among those badly wounded; in fact, the British officer who was attending him felt that Brugha would be dead by the following morning. However, he was taken to Mercer's Hospital, beside the College of Surgeons, where some twenty-three wounds had to be dressed and treated.

Still armed, Ceannt and his command marched to Jameson's Distillery in Marrowbone Lane. The Volunteers in Jameson's had made an unsuccessful attempt to contact Ceannt on Sunday morning. Thomas MacDonagh had informed them on his return journey from the meeting with Ceannt of the order to surrender, but they decided to remain alert as they had not heard from their commandant. They had in fact heard an unofficial report of the surrender the previous day but had doubts about its authenticity. In fact, the Volunteers in Jameson's Distillery must have been confident of some measure of victory because Con Colbert told the Cumann na mBan women that he was going to arrange a meal and a ceilidhe for them when the rebellion was over. Nevertheless, all doubts and uncertainties were dispelled when Ceannt arrived leading the garrison from the South Dublin Union. They stopped outside the distillery and Ceannt, accompanied by a British officer, went into the building and with dignity informed the rebels of the unconditional surrender.[9]

Ceannt ordered Séamus Murphy to have the garrison assembled and ready to move out. Séamus, assisted by Con Colbert, prepared the men and had them line up in military formation in the distillery yard. While his orders were being carried out, Ceannt spoke briefly with Lily. He advised her to return home at the first opportunity and gave her some money to give to Áine with a message telling her not to worry about him. Lily then joined her comrades in Cumann na mBan who were preparing to march out with the men. During the week Lily had kept a diary of events and of individual actions carried out by the Volunteers. However, she destroyed the document on the way to Richmond Barracks because she feared it might be incriminating if it was to fall into British hands. When all the Volunteers in the distillery had assembled, they marched out and joined the South Dublin Union garrison. Both garrisons then lined up together and began their march to Richmond Barracks.[10]

The column of prisoners was marched first to Bride Street where a large force of British military and army lorries awaited them. After the British commanding officer spoke with Ceannt, the order to disarm was given. The Volunteers immediately laid down their arms and equipment on the ground and took four paces back. The military then collected it in handcarts and brought the men to the waiting lorries. One of the priests, Fr Augustine, who was present for the surrender of the arms, later described the events from his perspective:

They did not arrive and I began to wonder what was causing the delay. In about fifteen minutes, however, we saw the South Dublin Union Garrison marching in, and at once my eye caught sight of the [magnificent] figure of the leader.

The whole column marched splendidly with guns slung from their left shoulders and their hands swinging freely at their sides. They wore no look of defeat, but rather of victory. It seemed as if they had come out to celebrate a triumph and were marching to receive a decoration. Ceannt was in the middle of the front [row] with one man on either side. But my eyes were riveted on him so tall was his form, so noble his bearing, and so manly his stride. He was indeed the worthy captain of a brave band who had fought a clean fight for Ireland.

They drew up just opposite us as we stood at the corner where [Bride] Street meets [Ross] Street and grounded their guns at his command. Father Aloysius and myself looked on in silence. We saw Éamonn give up his gun and then his belt to an English officer. But when I saw them take his Volunteer uniform I said to Father Aloysius: 'I can't stand this any longer. Come along and we'll let them see what we think of those men.' We walked across the street, shook hands warmly with Ceannt and with a 'Goodbye and God bless you' just looked at the officers and departed for Church Street after a tense and trying day.

(The words in square brackets in the above statement

were faded or missing from the original manuscript. However, Nurse Elizabeth O'Farrell later recorded that the Volunteers laid down their arms at the junction of the above streets.)

The prisoners were then marched towards Kilmainham and on to Richmond Barracks. During the march, the streets were lined with soldiers and there was some hostility towards the prisoners from bystanders. Nevertheless there were also words of encouragement, particularly as they passed the home of the Cosgrave family where loud cheering and clapping erupted for the rebels. The Cumann na mBan women who were marching at the rear of the column began singing rebel songs; Lily later wrote that they 'sang every rebel song known to them'.[11]

18

Court Martial

When the column reached Richmond Barracks, the prisoners were marched into the square. The women of Cumann na mBan were then separated from the rest of the garrison. By now the morale of the men was beginning to fade and one young Volunteer, Con Donovan, asked Ceannt to whistle a tune called 'The Blackbird', which he promptly did. The Volunteers were split up into indiscriminate groups and roughly hustled into rooms which had space for about twenty people. The doors were then locked and guards placed outside. Prior to their arrival, 200 other prisoners had been removed from Richmond Barracks and were on their way to internment camps in England. During the night, the stench from a bucket used as a toilet was overwhelming and Ceannt asked the guards to empty it, but his request fell on deaf ears. He then proceeded to open one of the windows but a sentry shut it immediately, saying he would shoot anyone attempting to open the window. The following morning Ceannt ordered his men to do some exercises as they did not know how long they would be confined. At noon all prisoners were marched to the gymnasium and told to sit on the floor. Volunteers from other battalions around the city were already assembled there. Ceannt saw John MacBride and made his way over to him to shake his hand, saying that he did not expect to see him in this particular detention centre, but said that he was not surprised that he had taken part in the rebellion. A short time later, detectives from Dublin Castle arrived and began to pick out the Volunteer leaders. Before he was separated from his men, Ceannt asked the British authorities to take special care of one man who he said had lost his sense of reason because of the fighting.[1]

Michael Kent was shocked at the sudden surrender, but because of the on-going military activities near his home was sure that hostilities would resume. Because of this, he prepared to leave the area and began to consolidate his finances, collecting all of the ready cash, some gold, life insurance policies and a post office savings book. His wife, Julia, stuffed the remaining flour, bread, sugar and tinned food into two pillowcases. However, before they could leave, a large force of cavalry and two large field guns passed the house at about 3 p.m. and by this time the area was already cordoned off by the military.

All day Sunday Áine and Mrs Brugha waited eagerly for any information, but none came. On Monday 1 May both women became extremely anxious for news and ventured out, but without much success, and were about to return to the house when they met a priest in the Rathmines area. He told them that the Volunteers would be interned and that the leaders were to be tried by court martial under the Defence of the Realm Act. Although she had been aware of her husband's role in the rebellion, Áine was still shocked by the news. The priest noticed the frightened reaction on Áine's face and tried to comfort her by suggesting that the situation might not be as dangerous as he believed. That day General Maxwell issued a manifesto declaring that the most rigorous measures would be taken against the rebels. He stated that, if necessary, he would not hesitate to destroy all buildings within a rebel-occupied area and warned residents they would have to evacuate such areas. Paying tribute to his troops, Maxwell had special praise for the battalion of Sherwood Foresters saying that 'the work they had to do was the most distasteful task ever asked of a soldier'. In a memorandum sent by General Maxwell to the British prime minister, H. H. Asquith, he provided the following description of Éamonn Ceannt:

> This man was one of the signatories to the Declaration of Irish Independence. He was on the Executive Committee and Central Council of the Irish Volunteers and attended all their meetings. He was an extremist in his views and identified himself with all pro-German movements. He held the rank of Commandant in the rebel army and was in command at the South Dublin Union in the capture of which the British troops suffered heavily, losing both officers and men. He was armed at the time of his surrender.[2]

THE COLLAPS[

REBEL LEADERS
SURRENDER.

THREE PRINCIPALS
TRIED AND SHOT.

OTHERS ARRESTED & HELD FOR
TRIAL UNCONDITIONALLY.

SERIOUS FIGHTING ALL ROUND THE CITY

HEAVY CASUALTIES IN DEAD AND
WOUNDED.

CENTRE OF DUBLIN DEVASTATED BY FIRE:
PALATIAL BUILDINGS IN ASHES.

The Sinn Fein insurrection, which broke out in Dublin City on Easter Monday at noon, has been effectively quelled.

The positions of vantage which the rebels took up in various parts of the city were reduced, and the leaders unconditionally surrendered.

Thomas J. Clarke, P. H. Pearse, and Thomas Macdonagh, three of the signatories to the poster proclaiming an Irish Republic, have been tried by court-martial and shot. The dead body of The O'Rahilly was found in Moore lane, adjacent to the G.P.O. James Connolly, Larkin's chief lieutenant, is wounded and a prisoner, F. Sheehy Skeffington has been shot.

The centre of the city has suffered severely from fire. The beautiful shops on one of the finest thoroughfares in Europe, Lr. O'Connell street, are a shapeless mass of ruins, while most of Henry street, Middle Abbey street, Earl street, and Prince's street and Eden quay, is in a similar condition.

No approximate estimate even of the casualties suffered by the military, the rebels, and civilians is available, but the number of deaths is large, and the people injured very numerous.

The monetary cost of the short-lived "rising" runs into many millions.

Sporadic attempts were made in different parts of the country to follow the example of Dublin, but the authorities report that they were promptly quelled, and that everything is settling down. In Meath a District Inspector and six policemen were killed and 15 police wounded.

DIARY OF EVENTS. the provision shops on the North side of the city were "sold out."

The *Irish Independent*, dated 25 April to 4 May reporting on the collapse of the rebellion and the execution of Clarke, Pearse and MacDonagh.

Court martial for the leaders began almost immediately with many of those who were found guilty of rebellion being sentenced to death. On Wednesday 3 May the executions began and the first to face the firing squad were Patrick Pearse, Thomas Clarke and Thomas MacDonagh. The following day, Edward Daly, William Pearse, Michael O'Hanrahan and Joseph Mary Plunkett were put to death. Plunkett married his fiancée, Grace Gifford, just hours before his execution. On Thursday morning, 4 May, the papers brought the news of the execution of Pearse, MacDonagh and Clarke. It was distressing news for Áine, with Ceannt's court martial pending. Nevertheless, she felt that another newspaper report carried a glimmer of hope when it stated that the House of Commons declared that a sentence of three years penal servitude would be imposed on Ceannt and three others. Although Áine was delighted with this news, she felt a great sense of sorrow for the men who had already been executed. She was particularly concerned over Thomas MacDonagh who she believed had not become deeply involved until shortly before the rebellion. Later that morning Ceannt and Seán Heuston faced separate courts martial. Those presiding over Ceannt's court martial included Brigadier-General C. G. Blackader (president), Lieutenant-Colonel G. German and Lieutenant-Colonel W. J. Kent. The charges against Ceannt were as follows:

> Did take part in an armed rebellion and in waging war against His Majesty the King, such act being of such a nature as to be calculated to be prejudicial to the Defence of the Realm and being done with the intention of and for the purpose of assisting the enemy.[3]

During proceedings, a barrister, Ronayne, was allowed to advise Ceannt. The first witness to give evidence was Major J. A. Armstrong who recalled that he was in Patrick's Park on 30 April 1916 when his troops came under fire from the neighbourhood of Jacob's Factory. He said that they sustained several casualties. He also stated that he was present when the rebels in Jacob's Factory surrendered and stated, 'The accused surrendered as one of the party and was at the head of it.' Lists of armed and unarmed rebels had been compiled and he went on to say that Ceannt's name was at the head of an armed list and that he described himself as a commandant. Major Armstrong then said that he requested the accused to give orders to his men, which he did, and these were obeyed. When cross-examined by Ceannt, Major Armstrong confirmed that the two lists of men, armed and unarmed, were compiled after the rebels were disarmed. Armstrong stated that the accused did not have a rifle but a revolver or automatic pistol which he removed from a pocket and placed on the ground.[4]

Éamonn Ceannt requested that three witnesses should be called in his defence: John MacBride, Richard Davys and Patrick Sweeney. Another witness he wished to call was Thomas MacDonagh, but he had been already executed. The first witness called by Ceannt in his defence was John MacBride. MacBride said that he knew the accused personally and was in no doubt as to his identity. MacBride then said that he had been in Jacob's Factory on 30 April 1916 and the preceding days and at no time did he see Éamonn Ceannt. He went on to say that it was impossible for the accused to have been in Jacob's Factory without his knowledge and added that Éamonn Ceannt had no connection with the party that occupied Jacob's Factory. When MacBride was cross-examined, he stated that he saw the accused in the area of St Patrick's Park when the group under his command surrendered, but that he did not see the accused at any time between Easter Monday and Sunday 30 April 1916. He also confirmed that he had no knowledge of the accused being in command of the Fourth Battalion. Both Richard Davys and Patrick Sweeney confirmed that they had not seen the accused in Jacob's Factory. However, Davys then stated that he had seen the accused in the area of St Patrick's Park. Following the evidence given by his last witness Éamonn Ceannt made this statement:

Three witnesses who were in Jacob's Factory from Monday 24 April 1916 to about 5 p.m. on Sunday 30 April have sworn that I was not in Jacob's Factory during any of that period and was not one of a party which surrendered from Jacob's Factory on Sunday 30 April. Another witness who was not available, Thomas MacDonagh, would have been able to corroborate these three. The evidence makes it quite clear that I can't have had anything to do with the firing from the neighbourhood of Jacob's which resulted in casualties to British troops at St Patrick's Park as referred to. I don't accuse Major Armstrong of endeavouring to mislead the court but it's clear that he was deceived in thinking that I was attached in any way to the Jacob's party which as deposed fired on British troops in the neighbourhood of Patrick's Park. He had admitted that his plan of making a list of armed men was by a process of elimination of the unarmed men from the whole list on parade and from recollection. He had admitted that the list of armed men was compiled after all men had been disarmed. I submit that this evidence is not conclusive except insofar as it concerned the unarmed men and is not evidence as to the men who were armed. I claim at least that there is reasonable doubt and the benefit of the doubt should be given to the accused. In regard to my carrying arms there is no positive or direct evidence except that Major Armstrong believes I carried a revolver or automatic pistol which he says I took from my pocket and laid upon the ground. As to my having surrendered to the military authorities this is sufficiently proved by my presence at Richmond Barracks and is hereby freely admitted. As to the accusation that I did an act '… with the intention and for the purpose of assisting the enemy …' I content myself with a simple denial. The Crown did not even tender evidence in this regard. I gave away my automatic pistol. The Volunteer uniform more often than not does not indicate the rank of the wearer. The witness I intended to call and could not be found from the description I gave to the Police would have proven that I did not come from the neighbourhood of Jacob's Factory. I came at the head of two bodies of men but was only connected with one body.[5]

When the court martial was over, Ronayne told the family that he admired Ceannt's composure during the trial and that he had defended his actions extremely well. The verdict of the court martial was that Éamonn Ceannt was guilty and he was sentenced to death by shooting, which was confirmed by General Maxwell. It is unclear why he was accused of leading the rebellion at Jacob's Factory when even Maxwell's letter to the prime minister (mentioned above), states his location during the rebellion: '[he] was in command at the South Dublin Union.'

During the day, Ceannt wrote two letters to Áine. One of the letters was obviously written while the court martial was in recess; the other seems to indicate a resignation to his fate. Ceannt made very few notes during the proceedings, but those he did make were written on the charge sheet:

Richmond Barracks
My wife at present at 5 Fitzwilliam Terrace, Dartry Road, Upper Rathmines.
Trial about to be resumed at 10 this (Thursday) 4th May '16
I am cheerful and happy and hope Áine and little Rónán also are so. Whatever befalls I shall try to accept my fate like a man and commend you and Rónán to the sympathy and support of our relatives and friends. Slán leat. Do not fret.
Éamonn Ceannt

Richmond Barracks
4/5/16
My wife, at present at 5 Fitzwilliam Terrace, Dartry Road, Upper Rathmines.
The gold watch in my possession give to Mrs Burgess.
The other things are yours to use as you think fit and this is to authorise the military authorities to hand all my things over to you. I have £2 in notes and about 12/– or 15/– in silver. Also a beads [rosary].
Éamonn Ceannt

On Friday morning, 5 May, Major John MacBride was executed. William Cosgrave and Thomas Hunter (another Volunteer officer) were also to face the firing squad, but their sentences were commuted to penal servitude for life. In the afternoon, Áine and Mrs Brugha went to visit Cathal Brugha in Mercer's Hospital. On the return journey, Áine went to visit her home in Dolphin Terrace, only to find the interior utterly destroyed, having been twice raided by the military, on 27 April and again on 1 May. When Áine returned to Fitzwilliam Terrace, her sister-in-law Nell had arrived to see how Áine and Rónán were bearing up. Áine was still hoping that her husband's life would be spared and she even wrote to the House of Commons requesting confirmation of the newspaper reports of amnesty. Nell suggested that they should call on the priests attending the condemned men, Fr Albert and Fr Augustine, at Church Street, who Nell felt sure would have reliable information. Fr Albert did not have any information but advised Áine not to pin her hopes on rumours. By this time it was very late and Áine decided against returning to Fitzwilliam Terrace, remaining instead at Nell's home in Drumcondra. Nell also told Áine that even though a military escort had been sent for Mrs MacDonagh to take her to say goodbye to her husband, she had failed to reach him in time. Bearing this in mind, Áine said that she would stay up all night if necessary.[6]

That day Ceannt, still unaware of his fate, wrote another two letters to Áine. There is some confusion as to when

Ceannt was actually transferred to Kilmainham Gaol. However, it is most likely that he was moved on the Friday evening. His second letter had the words Richmond Barracks crossed out and replaced with the word Kilmainham. Another indication that his transfer took place on Friday is the fact that Áine visited him in Kilmainham on Saturday.

Letter from Richmond Barracks
Richmond Barracks
5 May, 1916.

To my wife at present at 5 Fitzwilliam Terrace, Dartry Road, Upper Rathmines, or c/o Mr Richard Kent, 71 Richmond Road, Drumcondra.

Writing in English to say I am well but expecting the worst – which may be the best. Everyone amazingly cheerful and resigned to their several fates. Can see there is a 'reign of terror' outside.

Everyone seems to be here in Richmond Barracks. Lily probably in Kilmainham. I saw her. Not much comfort here, but I sleep well and we get ample rations. Make Mrs B's mind easy. I'm sure she's worrying. Tell Rónán to be a good boy and remember Easter 1916 for ever. I'm in excellent form. I'm sure all relatives etc., will be looked after later on. Don't expect you'll see No. 2 as you left it. Probably looted by this. Adieu or au revoir – I don't know which.

Mr M. A. Corrigan, Solr., 3 St Andrew St (undertakers also) might get you or Richard to see me.
Éamonn Ceannt.

5/5/1916, 4 p.m. Richmond Barracks

Áine (my wife)
Trial closed. I expect the death sentence which better men have already suffered. I only regret that I have now no longer an opportunity of showing how I think of you now that the chance of seeing you again is so remote. I shall die like a man for Ireland's sake.
Éamonn Ceannt.[7]

19

Execution

Early on Saturday morning Áine went to see a family friend, Johnny Foley, who had been secretary to the lord mayor of Dublin for many years. He went over to the Mansion House to see if anything could be done to help Áine gain access to Ceannt. He was informed that if they went to Richmond Barracks they would be admitted. As it was still very early, about 8.30 a.m., Áine decided to collect her mother and Rónán at Fitzwilliam Terrace and move them to Nell's house. After breakfast, Johnny Foley, Richard Kent and Áine drove to Richmond Barracks and met with the provost marshal, Viscount Powerscourt. Áine's memory immediately shot back to St Patrick's Day when she had observed Powerscourt watching Ceannt as he prepared the Volunteers for inspection at College Green. Viscount Powerscourt was very amiable towards them and said that he did not know the outcome of Ceannt's trial but agreed to give Áine a note for the governor of Kilmainham, where he had been moved, which would permit her to see her husband. They then drove to Kilmainham and, having produced the note from the viscount, Áine was admitted and taken to cell 88 in the central compound on the top landing where Ceannt was being held.

The couple immediately embraced and were silent for a few moments, not quite sure what to say to each other. Words of concern from Áine broke the silence as he held her in his arms. As she spoke, Áine stood back a little to look at her husband and noticed his Sam Browne that she had so lovingly polished on the morning of the rebellion was missing. It had been removed by the British military, but this did not take from his proud combatant appearance as he stood there in his slightly torn uniform gazing at the woman he loved. An army sergeant stood at the door while the couple spoke softly so it was difficult to express the intimate emotion they both felt. Áine also noticed that a wooden wall panel in the cell bore the pencilled inscription: 'Joseph Plunkett's cell – me – execution – out – a.m. May – (Signed) Grace Plunkett.' During their conversation Áine told Ceannt that the Rising had been an awful fiasco, but he replied: 'No, it was the biggest thing since '98.' Before she left the cell, Ceannt gave her Cathal Brugha's watch to give to his wife; John Joyce had given the watch to him prior to the surrender. Grasping her hand he then gave her the remainder of his money and they again embraced. As she was leaving, Áine made him promise that he would send for her regardless of the situation, as this was no time for trying to spare her emotions.[1]

Ceannt certainly knew the verdict of the court martial

by 4 p.m. on Sunday 7 May as it was on that day that he wrote his statement regarding the rebellion. Sometime during the day he was transferred to cell 20 on the ground floor of the central compound, possibly to make it more convenient for the military to take him to the execution yard on Monday morning. He attended mass in the jail that day and this was the last time that Lily O'Brennan saw him. She remembered him holding his rosary beads and receiving holy communion along with Colbert, Heuston and Mallin. As they were leaving, Lily waved to him. She never forgot the calm detached look on his face and later recalled that he seemed on the 'rim of eternity, I felt his fate was sealed'. When she returned to her cell, she confided her worst fears to her companion but was reassured that he would not be executed.

Later one of the guards came into Ceannt's cell and gave him a piece of cake he had smuggled in. Ceannt recognised him immediately as a young soldier whom he had allowed to escape in the South Dublin Union. The soldier was totally unaware of just how close he had come to being killed by the prisoner now in his custody. Ceannt mentioned this incident in his rebellion statement. While awaiting execution, Ceannt wrote a number of short notes and letters, among them a note to the commandant of Kilmainham detailing his belongings. To Áine and Rónán he wrote in the language he loved so dearly:

Nóta dá Bhean chéile, 7 Bhealtaine, 1916
Date 7/5/16
Time 4 p.m.
Place (Kilmainham)
To, Áine, Mo bhean,
Coinnigh é seo i gcuimhne a Áine a mhíle ghradh.
Abair le Rónán go bhfuilim ag fághail bháis ar son na hÉireann.
Nuair a thiocfas ciall agus tuigsint aige tuigfidh sé an méid sin.
Dulce et decorum est pro patria mori.
Seo é an 7adh lá de Mhí na Bealtaine 1916.
From Éamonn Ceannt.

[Keep this in mind Áine my dear love. Tell Rónán I'm dying for Ireland. When he gets sense and wisdom he will understand that much. Sweet is death for one's country. This is the 7th day of May 1916.]

i bPríosún Chille Maighnean
Nóta dá Bhean chéile, 7 Bhealtaine, 1916
Dom' Mhaicín bhocht Rónán,
Ón a athair atá ar tí bás d'fhághail amáireach ar son an h-Éireann.
Slán agus beannacht.
Éamonn Ceannt.

I.S. Tabhair aire mhaith dho do mháithrín. Go gcúidighidh Dia an bheirt agaibh, agus go dtugaidh Sé saoghal fada faoi shogh agus faoi mhaise dhaoibh araon.
Go saoraidh Dia Éire.

[In Kilmainham Jail
7 May, 1916
To my poor little son Rónán,
From his father who is going to die tomorrow for the sake of Ireland.
Goodbye and blessings.
Éamonn Ceannt.
P.S. Take good care of your mother. May God help you both and may he give you both a long and fulfilled life.
May God free Ireland.]

Proposed Arrangements for Áine:
Cell No. 20
Kilmainham Jail
7th May, 1916.
Arrangements for Áine (proposed)
(1) To take my place re weekly collections as long as they are remunerative.
(2) To have my two Insurances looked after. I leave all my possessions to my wife.
(3) Perhaps the D.M.O.A. would make a grant.
(4) Richard to apply for assistance out of any Fund which may be organised for the relief of dependents.
(5) For the above purpose – (4) – to communicate with J. R. Reynolds, An Cumann Urudhais, College Street, who may be able to give information or guidance.
(6) I leave my watch-chain to Rónán subject to his mother's approval. Also, if she approves, I would like Mick, Richard, Nell, Lily, Mrs Brennan, John P. and Bill to get each some small token of me with my blessing.
Éamonn.

He also left the following note:

> Fágaim mo bheannacht ag na daoine seo thíos uile.
> [I leave my greetings/blessings to all of those listed below].
> Capt. Séamus Murphy, formerly of 7 St Mary's Terrace, Rathfarnham
> John P. Kent my brother and Colr. Sergeant William Kent
> Joe Crofts 82 Lr. Camden Street
> Mrs Mellows 21 Mountshannon Road
> Lily Brennan with best wishes for the future
> Seán Mac Giobúin c/o Corporation
> Miss Crissie Doyle; Mary Nolan Buttevant.[2]

On Sunday evening Áine went to see Sir Charles Cameron on Raglan Road. She inquired about the newspaper report which referred to the sentence of three years, saying that she did not believe that the report was genuine. She asked Sir Charles if anything could be done to save her husband and, although it was very late, he promised to do his best. On her return to Nell's house at Drumcondra it started to rain so when she arrived she went straight to one of the back rooms to dry herself. Suddenly there was a loud knock on the front door. Nell's husband Jack came into the room and told her that there was a soldier looking for her at the door. Áine went out immediately to meet him only to learn that he was on leave from Fermoy and was a friend of Éamonn Ceannt's brother, William, who at that time was stationed in Fermoy, County Cork. William had asked the soldier to call on Áine and the others to inquire about their safety. Having given the soldier some light refreshment, they proceeded to tell him about the events of Easter Week. The soldier then informed them that William was also in some difficulty and was to be court-martialled on the charge of stealing food from the military canteen and giving it to a nationalist prisoner named Thomas Kent (no relation). William insisted that he had purchased the food. The outcome of the court martial is not known, although William did remain in the service of the king. The soldier then left and Áine and the others settled down around the fire discussing what might happen. By now, Áine was becoming very anxious and upset. She had never really let the consequences of a failed rebellion cloud her mind but now it was all too real.[3]

At about ten o'clock there was another knock at the door. This time it was an army officer delivering a note from Ceannt, stating that he wished to see Áine. When Áine went outside, Ceannt's brother Richard was already in the officer's car. She climbed in and the officer drove off immediately to collect Michael. When they reached Kilmainham, they handed in their letters and were registered. Lanterns were procured and they were led 'down the dark corridors into the bowels of this hellish abode'. Soon the rattle of keys signalled their arrival at Ceannt's cell. As they entered, he rose to greet them and shook their hands quite calmly. Having exchanged a few words, he put his arms around Áine, bent his head and, smiling sweetly, kissed her tenderly. Their embrace was more intense than it had been during her earlier visit. They were lovers again, and all present knew that they needed those few moments together. Michael and Richard turned towards the sentries, to give Ceannt and Áine some degree of privacy and conversed quietly. Áine and Ceannt remained standing for some minutes and then sat on the edge of the low plank bed in the corner. Once again Áine noticed her surroundings; the new cell contained a couple of boards on which she presumed Ceannt rested. There was also a chair and a makeshift desk on which a lighted candle stood. Through the candlelight she noted there was a pen and ink. Áine asked how he was doing mentally and he replied that he was quite prepared to walk and face the firing squad at quarter to four in the morning, but that all the rumours of a reprieve had disturbed him. As there had not been any executions since Friday when MacBride had been shot, some of the soldiers were saying that anything could happen.[4]

A few minutes before they left, Ceannt called them all around him for a last chat. As there was no seating they knelt down and he spoke to them in a very matter-of-fact way. He said that one of the priests had said that there was a chance of a reprieve and again that some soldiers were also hinting at this. Ceannt was evidently trying to avoid any scene of heartbreak and was trying to console Áine and his brothers. Michael later said that his voice was somewhat strained, but that he never saw him look so well. He was wearing the green uniform of the Irish Volunteers, his moustache was neatly trimmed and his face had a tanned and healthy look about it. During the conversation Ceannt took two letters from his pocket, one of which was for Áine to read to Rónán, telling him that he had died for Ireland, and the other was the note on the charge sheet. After about twenty minutes the sentry made a gesture that time was up and kindly told them that they would have to leave. They all stood up and Ceannt told them that he had asked to see Fr Augustine, but that he had not arrived. Richard said this to the sentry, who offered to take him to the commandant to inquire about the priest which seemed to please Ceannt. They each shook Ceannt's hand heartily and Richard told him not to worry about Áine, as he would look after her. Ceannt again embraced Áine and kissed her for the last time.

Michael waited back a moment to tell Ceannt that the rebellion had not been in vain and that a huge sum of money had already been raised in America for the Irish cause. Finally Michael said, 'We'll go home and pray for you till 4 a.m. in the morning', to which Ceannt answered, 'Aye, do.' From outside the cell, Michael looked back despondently at his younger brother. Inside the cell Ceannt stood with the candlelight clearly highlighting his features through the semi-darkness. He was looking down at the little makeshift table where he had been writing, silently wrapped in thought, a deep furrow formed on his brow. Michael carried this memory with him for the remainder of his life.[5]

As they were about to leave Kilmainham, the commandant told Richard that he had sent for Fr Augustine and that he would be with Ceannt shortly. He also said to him: 'There is no reprieve. Go back and tell your brother.' Richard did so, but did not tell Áine until the following day after the sentence had been carried out. Having heard that his execution would go ahead at dawn, Ceannt maintained his composure, shook his brother's hand, embraced him and said farewell. Alone again, he now had only hours to make his peace with God and write a farewell letter to his wife. It was also time to make his will:

> Kilmainham Gaol,
> 7th May, 1916.
> I hereby leave all I have in the world to my wife to do with same whatever she thinks fit. (Would she please give my watch-chain to Rónán.)
> Éamonn Ceannt

In the early hours of Monday morning, 8 May, Fr Augustine arrived to minister to Ceannt. Upon entering the cell he noticed the sheet of writing paper. Fr Augustine spoke with him for a while and later wrote of the encounter:

> But let me take only one man and tell you his story. The only man I shall take from the number, and whose name strangely stirs me now, is the brave, the gallant, the glorious, and upright Éamonn Ceannt. Father, you have to make other visits, haven't you? Yes said I, I have. Well Father, said he, I would like you to come back to me again. And then taking

out his watch, he looked at it and said: Father, I have yet another hour, have I not? And I turned to the wall before I said: Yes Éamonn, just another hour.

After Fr Augustine had left, Ceannt began to write his last letter to Áine:

2.30a.m.

8/5/16

My dearest wife Áine,

Not wife but widow before these lines reach you. I am here without hope of this world and without fear, calmly awaiting the end. I have had Holy Communion and Fr Augustine has been with me and will be back again. Dearest 'silly little Fanny'. My poor little sweetheart of many years ago. Ever my comforter, God comfort you now. What can I say? I die a noble death, for Ireland's freedom. Men and women will vie with one another to shake your dear hand. Be proud of me as I am and ever was of you. My cold exterior was but a mask. It has saved me these last days. You have a duty to me and to Rónán, that is to live. My dying wishes are that you shall remember your state of health, work only as much as may be necessary and freely accept the little attentions which in due time will be showered upon you. You will be, you are, the wife of one of the Leaders of the Revolution. Sweeter still you are my little child, my dearest pet, my sweetheart of the hawthorn hedges and Summers' eves. I remember all and I banish all that I may be strong and die bravely. I have one hour to live, then God's judgment and, through his infinite mercy, a place near your poor Grannie and my mother and father and Jem and all the fine old Irish Catholics who went through the scourge of

similar misfortune from this Vale of Tears into the Promised
Land. Bíodh misneach agat a stoirín mo chroidhe. Tóig do
cheann agus bíodh foighde agat go bhfeicfimíd a cheile arís i
bhFlaithis Dé, tusa, mise agus Rónán beag beag bocht.
[Be hopeful love of my heart. Keep your head and be patient
until we see each other again in God's Heaven, yourself,
myself and poor little Rónán.]
Adieu
Éamonn.[6]

The other revolutionaries who were to be executed that
same morning were Michael Mallin, Con Colbert and Seán
Heuston. Fr Augustine returned to Ceannt after visiting
Michael Mallin. He gave Fr Augustine two letters – one was
to Áine and the other was his statement on the rebellion. He
then made his peace with God, praying for the support of all
the Irish saints. Before leaving him again, Fr Augustine gave
him a crucifix, saying, 'Ceannt, keep that, and I will be with
you to the last.' Shortly after Fr Augustine left, the military
arrived and told Ceannt that his time had come. He stood
to attention as one of the soldiers tied his hands behind his
back. They marched him, still grasping the crucifix, to the
stone-breakers yard as dawn was breaking. On the way he
met Fr Augustine who was rushing back to be with him. Fr
Augustine's memories of Éamonn Ceannt's last moments
were very vivid:

I saw Éamonn coming towards me down the hall, and my
soul leaped to him, and my heart embraced him, and we

went out together, he to die for Ireland, and I to live for my country.

When they reached the place of execution, Fr Augustine said to him, 'When you fall Éamonn, I'll run over and anoint you', to which he answered: 'Oh that will be a great consolation Father.' He was then blindfolded and the twelve-man firing squad, six standing, six kneeling, was placed under orders by the commanding officer. Fr Augustine stood a short distance away and watched as Ceannt was made to sit on a soapbox and asked to stretch out his legs. He still held the crucifix tightly, his knuckles white and, while he was forgiving his enemies, the firing squad took their aim and fired. His last words were, 'My Jesus, mercy.' He tumbled from the soapbox, but a spark of life still burned making it necessary for the commanding officer to administer the *coup de grâce*. Fr Augustine rushed over to Ceannt's body and removed the blood-splattered crucifix from his hands.[7]

When Michael arrived home, he asked his family to kneel before a statue of the Sacred Heart and in his own words, 'I prayed on as I never prayed before.' Michael continued to pray alone after the others had retired for the night and from time to time he would go into the front room to peep out of the window to witness a very significant approaching dawn. His prayers continued and soon afterwards in the perfect stillness of the morning, he remembered:

I heard clearly the faint click of a rifle; 'twas faint, but in that solemn stillness perfectly distinct. Instantly my whole nerves seemed to contract up into my heart, and I pulled out my watch – seven minutes to four. I felt I knew then definitely that all was over with poor Éamonn. I put out the lights and went upstairs and into bed. I cried bitterly from the depths of my heart. But God's will be done.

Meanwhile back at Nell's home, Áine had refused to rest, deciding to remain awake all night. Nell was also very restless and had decided to stay awake with Áine. As each hour passed, they knelt down and recited the rosary. They prayed continually from 3 a.m. until about 5.30 a.m. knowing that everything would definitely be over by then if indeed the execution had taken place. At 6 a.m., with curfew lifting, they made their way down to Church Street. It was a glorious summer morning and, upon arriving at the priory, they asked to see Fr Augustine. The priest who answered the door told them that Fr Augustine had been late arriving back from Kilmainham and that, having celebrated an early mass, he had retired to his room. He went on to say that, if they wished, that he would call him. Áine said not to disturb him but that she was anxious to hear any news of her husband, to which the priest replied, 'He is gone to Heaven.' Áine was inconsolable. Gone was the man she had loved since the first moment she saw him on the train to Galway all those years ago. Memories of the wonderful moments they had spent together flooded into her mind. She struggled to regain her composure and Nell tried to comfort her as they turned for home. On the return journey the two ladies made their way to Iona Church for 8 a.m. mass. There they met Richard who had already given Ceannt's name to the priest to have him remembered during mass. Richard then told Áine that he had known for sure since the previous night that the execution would take place. On returning to the house Áine's first duty was to inform Rónán. She went to the child's bedroom and explained gently to him that his father had been executed but that he had given his life for a great cause, the freedom of Ireland.[8]

At 10 a.m. both women paid another visit to Church Street, where they met with Fr Augustine. He told Áine that because of all the conflicting stories the previous week he had called to Sir John Maxwell a few days before the execution. He inquired if there was any truth in the rumour that the executions were finished. Maxwell sent out word to him that there was no truth in the rumours and that the executions would take place as planned. Fr Augustine then gave Áine and Nell the full details of Ceannt's last moments. Áine took great comfort in the knowledge that Fr Augustine had stayed with him until it was over. Fr Augustine then gave Áine the last two letters from Ceannt, the personal letter to herself and his rebellion statement.[9]

This 7 May statement from Kilmainham Gaol gives an insight into how he felt about the rebellion and how strongly he opposed the surrender. He obviously began writing the statement prior to being taken to Cell 20 as the document records his location as Cell 88:

Cell 88,

Kilmainham Gaol,

7 May, 1916.

I leave for the guidance of other Irish revolutionaries who may tread the path which I have trod this advice never to treat with the enemy, never to surrender to his mercy, but fight to a finish. I see nothing gained but grave disaster caused by the surrender which has marked the end of the Irish Insurrection of 1916 – so far at least as Dublin is concerned. The enemy has not cherished one generous thought for those who, with little hope, with poor equipment, and weak in numbers, withstood his forces for one glorious week. Ireland has shown she is a Nation. This generation can claim to have raised sons as brave as any that went before. And in the years to come Ireland will honour those who risked all for her honour at Easter in 1916. I bear no ill will towards those against whom I have fought. I have found the common soldiers and the higher officers human and companionable, even the English who were actually in the fight against us. Thank God soldiering for Ireland has opened my heart and made me see poor humanity where I expected to see only scorn and reproach. I have met the man who escaped from me by a rush under the Red Cross. But I do not regret having withheld my fire. He gave me cakes!

I wish to record the magnificent gallantry and fearless calm determination of the men who fought with me. All, all, were simply splendid. Even I knew no fear nor panic and shrunk from no risk even as I shrink not now from the death which faces me at daybreak. I hope to see God's face for a moment in the morning. His will be done. All are very kind. My poor wife saw me yesterday and bore up – so my warden told me – even after she left my presence. Poor Áine, poor

Rónán. God is their only shield now that I am removed. And God is a better shield than I. I have just seen Áine, Nell, Richard and Mick and bade them a conditional goodbye. Even now they hope!
Éamonn Ceannt.[10]

20

Aftermath

A few days after Ceannt's execution, the House of Commons replied to Áine's letter relating to the newspaper report of Ceannt's sentence being commuted to life in prison:

> 9–5–16.
> Madam,
> The irregularity of the post due to the disturbances only brought me tonight your –? I much regret your sorrow, but no such statement was made by Mr Asquith. The newspaper gave –? Nevertheless I feel that had I received in time the fact that your hopes had been raised by even a misreport I could have gone to the Prime Minister and pleaded a wife's cause. No husband would have stood indifferent to it. Where love and death are concerned there is no nationality; – your argument as a woman went the whole way. It is my grief that I can only salute you as a widow.
> Jim Healy.[1]

(There are a number of words which cannot be clearly identified in the original document, so the missing words have been replaced with dashes. Respectively, the words were possibly 'request', 'an incorrect report', and 'and'.)

Lily O'Brennan arrived home tired and dirty, having spent two weeks in Kilmainham Gaol without a change of clothes. Having been released, Lily and a friend went to visit Mrs Mellows in Mountshannon Road. The house had been raided by the military just before they arrived so the women decided it was possibly the safest place to stay that night. The following day Lily went to join Áine and told her of her experiences in Kilmainham. She also told of being awakened at dawn on a number of mornings by a volley of rifle shots, followed almost immediately by a single revolver shot. She said that she had heard the volley that sent Ceannt to the grave, but did not know it at the time. It was later that morning when a young woman outside the cell whispered the news of Ceannt's death. At first Lily cried out but she immediately took control of herself and began to recite a few quiet prayers for all those executed. Lily always had great admiration for Ceannt, but this was intensified upon hearing the account of his death.

Shortly after the rebellion, Martin Daly wrote the following about his old friend:

I saw – I maintain unashamed – I saw Destiny marked on that gentle brooding face, that profound forehead with something of the Bismarck or Old-Salisbury grandeur or gravity. I would venture the notion that of all those whom I personally knew of the men that died in the year 1916, Éamonn Ceannt was incomparably the most religious spirit:

I think he brooded mystically over something the others probably felt as passionately or more passionately, but he with a depth of ruminated conviction quite rare in the world. In all the others the enemy might assert – not truthfully but with a catching appearance of truth – that there was something a trifle hysterical or histrionic: of Ceannt this could never have been for one moment imagined: he was born to the remote tranquillity of a harvest moon.[2]

On 12 May Seán Mac Diarmada and James Connolly became the last men to be executed by firing squad. Because of his wounds, James Connolly had to be taken to his place of execution by stretcher-bearers. He was then propped up on a chair before the firing squad. Sir Roger Casement was tried for treason in London and, having been found guilty, was subsequently hanged at Pentonville prison on 3 August 1916. He was the last of the 1916 men to be executed and the only one to be hanged. On 1 March 1965, after a state funeral, the remains of Roger Casement were reinterred at Glasnevin Cemetery, Dublin.

After the rebellion, many of the Volunteers were rounded up and interned in England and Wales, among them Michael Collins. On 11 May Éamon de Valera's death sentence was commuted to life imprisonment. Eoin MacNeill was also court-martialled and imprisoned in Dartmoor for a year. Although there were mixed feelings among the Volunteers about MacNeill, they paid him the same respect as the other commanders. Upon his arrival in prison, Éamon de Valera stepped forward and called the

Volunteers to attention and MacNeill accepted the salute. On his release MacNeill joined the Sinn Féin government of 1918. He remained in politics until he lost his parliamentary seat in the 1927 election. He then returned to his academic career. Eoin MacNeill died in 1945, some say still haunted by the memory of Easter Week.

Arthur Griffith was also arrested after the rebellion and imprisoned, but was released before the end of that year. He became a member of the First Dáil of 1919. In 1921, he was part of the Irish delegation that returned to Dublin with the signed Anglo-Irish Treaty. Although a narrow majority passed the Treaty, the anti-Treaty IRA refused to accept it and civil war broke out. The Civil War was a bitter blow to Griffith and on 12 August 1922, he died of a brain haemorrhage.

Cathal Brugha eventually recovered from his wounds. He opposed the Anglo-Irish Treaty and joined the anti-Treaty forces in the Civil War. On 5 July 1922, Free State soldiers shot and fatally wounded Brugha in O'Connell Street, Dublin. He died two days later. William Cosgrave, who was a personal friend but political enemy of Cathal Brugha, paid a tribute to his dead friend, saying that he was 'the bravest man I ever knew'.

In 1920, Liam Mellows returned from America. He joined the republican side during the Civil War, for which he was arrested and imprisoned in Mountjoy Jail. On 8 December 1922, he was executed by Free State forces along with Rory O'Connor, Richard Barrett and Joseph

McKelvey. The executions took place in reprisal for the fatal shooting of Dáil Deputy, Seán Hales, in Dublin the previous day.[3]

The funerals at Glasnevin Cemetery, where most of the Rising's victims were brought for burial, produced many sad scenes. By 12 May 216 civilians had been buried in Glasnevin, twenty-nine in Dean's Grange Cemetery and nineteen in Mount Jerome Cemetery. In some cases, both British soldiers and rebel dead were buried in the same cemetery. Lieutenant Ramsay, one of the British officers killed while leading the charge on the South Dublin Union, was buried in Mount Jerome Cemetery. The remains of Nurse Kehoe, the woman killed in the South Dublin Union, were taken to Carlow for burial.[4]

People were also angry over reports of atrocities committed by the military. Major Sir Francis Vane, worried about the reputation of the British army, travelled to England and reported the dreadful actions of his fellow officer, Captain Bowen-Colthurst, who had been responsible for the unlawful killing of Francis Sheehy-Skeffington. Lord Kitchener did not act upon Vane's report, in fact the reverse happened: Sir Francis was deprived of his rank and dismissed from service. Justice was not served in this case until Prime Minister Asquith addressed the allegations. Bowen-Colthurst was then court-martialled, found guilty but insane, and incarcerated in Broadmoor criminal asylum. However, after a year he was released and he went on to become a successful banker in Vancouver. He died in

1965. Sir John Maxwell later admitted to the *Daily Mail* that brutalities had been committed. In fact, a war office document from June 1916, written by Sir Edward Troup, permanent secretary to the Home Department, referred to several cases of unarmed civilians being shot by British soldiers. These files were released in January 2001 and indicated that some soldiers were instructed that prisoners were not to be taken.

Although the Easter Rebellion failed from a military stand-point, it struck at the very heart of British colonialism in Ireland. One could easily exaggerate the effects of the rebellion, but it did ensure a measure of victory with the foundation of the Irish Free State. Attitudes to the rebellion soon shifted and after the last executions were carried out public opinion changed dramatically, from criticism of the rebels to admiration and support for them.[5]

The cost of the rebellion in human lives was over 1,351 killed or severely wounded, most of those being civilians. The cost in monetary terms was £2.5 million, with 179 buildings destroyed in central Dublin.[6]

Because of its ideals, the rebellion was now an embarrassment to the British government. After all, the Irish rebels had just fought and died for the same principles for which England had declared war against Germany: 'the freedom of small nations'. Asquith needed American support for the war in Europe and this could only be gained if he could convince America that there was an answer to the Irish question. He travelled to Dublin to assess the situation and instructed David Lloyd George to find a solution that would please all parties concerned. Lloyd George's scheme was to promise a more enduring settlement after the war but in the meantime to grant home rule for twenty-six counties. On the question of Ulster, he told John Redmond that Ulster's exclusion was only temporary. He then told Edward Carson that he did not want Ulster to merge with the rest of Ireland, thus pleasing both sides. As a show of good will, England began releasing the rebel prisoners and by July 1917 all prisoners were home. The Volunteers returned to Ireland and were welcomed as heroes, almost in total contrast to when they were marched away. The streets of Dublin were lined with republican flags – the memory of what the fallen leaders had sought to achieve now having a major effect on the ideals of Irish nationalism. By October Sinn Féin membership had increased to a quarter of a million and the commitment to independence was growing daily.

The following is a list of Irish Volunteers killed during, and as a result of, the Easter Rebellion:

John Adams	Thomas Allen	Frank Burke
Goban Burke	Andrew Byrne	Joseph Byrne
Charles Carrigan	Sir Roger Casement	Éamonn Ceannt
Philip Clarke	Thomas Clarke	Con Colbert
James Connolly	Seán Connolly	James Corcoran
John Costello	Harry Coyle	John Crinigan
John Cromean	Edward Daly	Charles Darcy

Peter Darcy

John Dwan

James Fox

Seán Heuston

John Kealy

Richard Kent

John MacBride

Francis Macken

Michael Malone

William M'Dowell

D. Murray

John O'Grady

J. O'Reilly

J. Owens

Joseph Mary Plunkett

George Reynolds

Patrick Shortis

Thomas Weafer

Brendan Donelan

Edward Ennis

George Geoghegan

Seán Howard

Con Keating

Thomas Kent

Seán Mac Diarmada

Peter Macken

Peter Manning

D. Murphy

Richard O'Carroll

Michael O'Hanrahan

Richard O'Reilly

Patrick Pearse

James Quinn

Frederick Ryan

John Traynor

Patrick Whelan

Patrick Doyle

Patrick Farrell

John Healy

John Hurley

John Keily

Gerald Keogh

Thomas MacDonagh

Michael Mallin

J. McCormack

Richard Murphy

Patrick O'Flanagan

The O'Rahilly

Thomas O'Reilly

William Pearse

Thomas Rafferty

Domhnall Sheehan

Edward Walsh

Peter Wilson.[7]

Epilogue

Although Ceannt's death had a profound effect on Áine, she did not brood over her misfortune. Rather she gathered strength in the belief that by his death he had simply joined the ranks of Tone and Emmet. She felt that it was her duty to work hard for the ideals which had cost him his life. On 31 March 1917, Áine wrote a letter to British headquarters at Parkgate, Dublin, complaining about the two raids on their home the previous year and explaining that the house had been ransacked, furniture broken and personal items stolen, with estimated damage of £350. She insisted that the items be returned at once, including two swords, an old one which was found in the River Boyne and a parade sword; also a gold medal with Ceannt's name engraved on it; a photograph of him and a number of other items. In reply she was offered compensation for the items, but she refused saying that they could not be replaced with money. Soon after this correspondence her house was raided again by the military, ironically during Easter 1917. A short time later, the family received word that William Kent had been killed in action in France, almost on the first anniversary of the rebellion.[1]

Áine was later appointed honorary treasurer of Cumann

na mBan and became one of its four vice-presidents, a position she held until her retirement from the movement in 1924. In 1917, she was a delegate at Count Plunkett's convention and in October, was co-opted as a member of the standing or executive committee of Sinn Féin and was elected annually until 1924. In 1918, she was elected to Rathmines urban district council, and was elected vice-chairman of the council from 1920 to 1922. When the Irish White Cross was established in 1920, Áine became a member of its central council. This organisation looked after the interests of the child victims of the troubles in Ireland. Over 1,000 children were looked after and educated from funds set aside by this central council. In 1922, Áine became secretary of the Irish White Cross, a position she held until 1947. During the War of Independence, she was appointed by the Labour department to preside at arbitrations in various parts of the country during a time when travelling throughout the country was very difficult and dangerous.[2]

In December 1920, her home was raided again by the military. This time they did more serious damage to the property and Áine and other members of the family were held in the dining-room for three hours while the raid took place. Áine again followed this up with the military and this time identified the officer in charge during the raid. It seems that he was later court-martialled for his actions. In May 1921, the house was raided again and this time the officer in charge was very courteous but some of his men were drunk. One of them climbed into the attic and cracked the bedroom ceilings, actually falling through one of them. Later an officer apologised for the damage and said that he would report it to the senior military authorities. Her home was raided eleven times in all with shots being fired on three occasions and again many articles of personal and historic value being stolen.[3]

In 1921, Áine accepted the position of secretary of the General County Councils of Ireland. She used her free time to help with the establishment of communication lines for Sinn Féin throughout the country. While she was engaged in this work, a truce was declared in the War of Independence making Áine's position redundant. After the signing of the Anglo-Irish Treaty on 6 December 1921, Áine attended all meetings of the standing executive of Sinn Féin. In February 1922, Áine presided over the Cumann na mBan convention held in the Mansion House, Dublin. The convention was held to consider the Treaty, which was defeated at the meeting by an overwhelming majority of 419 to 63. According to Áine, Cumann na mBan was the first organisation to register its opinion. Áine took the republican side during the Civil War, but from December 1922 to April 1923, she was a member of a Sinn Féin peace committee, established to attempt to find a peaceful solution. When the Sinn Féin courts were established she acted as a district justice, first for the south Dublin city area and later for Rathmines and Rathgar.[4]

On Easter Sunday 1935, Áine attended the unveiling

of a memorial commemorating the rebellion at the GPO, and in 1966, Galway railway station was officially named the Éamonn Ceannt station, as part of the fiftieth anniversary celebrations of the rebellion. A plaque was unveiled by Josephine McNamara, *née* O'Keeffe, a former member of Cumann na mBan, who had served with the Fourth Battalion during the 1916 rebellion. At one stage Áine and Lily intended to write a biography of Ceannt, but this never materialised. Perhaps it was Lily's death in May 1948 that ended the idea.

When the central council of the Irish Red Cross was founded in 1939, the government nominated Áine as a member. She acted as honorary treasurer from its inception until 1947 when the pressure of this work compelled her to resign. She died in 1954 and was buried in Dean's Grange Cemetery.

Notes

The footnotes given below relate to whole paragraphs in the text, rather than to single points of information.

1 – THE RISE OF NATIONALISM

1. Crealey, A. H. (1993) *An Irish Almanac*, p. 64; Foster, R. F. (1989) *The Oxford Illustrated History of Ireland*, p. 365; Hayes-McCoy, G. A. (1990) *Irish Battles, A Military History of Ireland*, p. 270; Shepherd, R. (1990) *Ireland's Fate, The Boyne and After*, pp. 167, 185; *The Battle of Aughrim 1691*, Interpretative Centre Booklet.

2. Boylan, H. (1981) *Wolfe Tone*, pp. 19, 132–5; Crealey, *An Irish Almanac*, pp. 35, 123, 146; *The Battle of Aughrim 1691*.

3. Woodham-Smith, C. (1962) *The Great Hunger*, pp. 15–16, 18.

4. Crealey, *An Irish Almanac*, p. 35; Foster, *The Oxford Illustrated History of Ireland*, p. 363; Litton, H. (1994) *The Irish Famine, an Illustrated History*, pp. 7–8; O'Hara, B. (1984) *Michael Davitt Remembered*, pp. 2, 11; Shiel, M. and Roche, D. (1986) *A Forgotten Campaign, and Aspects of the Heritage of South East Galway*, pp. Editorial, 23, 25, 27.

5. Gallagher Family Manuscripts, Éamonn Ceannt (1881–1916) by David M. Ceannt.

2 – FROM BIRTH TO MANHOOD

1. Gallagher Family Manuscripts, 'Kent family profile' by Joan and Mary Gallagher; Registration of Births and Deaths in Ireland, District of Williamstown, Union of Glennamaddy, County Galway;

O'Neill, T. (1966), 'Éamonn Ceannt', *Wine and Gold*, pp. 25–6; Royal Irish Constabulary Register, Extract, Surrey, England; RTÉ Archives, television documentaries, 15 April 1966, 'On Behalf of the Provisional Government – Éamonn Ceannt' (97D00109) and 21 November 1965, 'Portraits 1916' (94D00029); National Library of Ireland Archives, Éamonn Ceannt (Miscellaneous Items), PC 166–666, Box 1, Folder 11 and Box 2, Folder 8, 19.

2. Extracts from the diary of Michael Kent; Gallagher Family Manuscripts, 'Éamonn Ceannt' by Lily O'Brennan; Moira Kent Manuscripts, 'Account of Éamonn Ceannt' by Richard Ceannt; O'Neill, *Wine and Gold*, pp. 25–6; Royal Irish Constabulary Register, Extract, Surrey, England; National Library of Ireland Archives, Box 2, Folder 7, 8, 19.

3. Allen Library Archives, 'Edward T. Kent's Diary 1897–1898', pp. 4, 12, 23; Gallagher Family Manuscripts, 'Éamonn Ceannt' by Lily O'Brennan; O'Neill, *Wine and Gold* pp. 25–6; National Library of Ireland Archives, Box 2, Folder 8 and Éamonn Ceannt P2283.

4. Gallagher Family Manuscripts, 'Kent family profile' by Joan and Mary Gallagher; Moira Kent Manuscripts, 'Notes on Éamonn Ceannt' by Richard Ceannt; *The Galway Express*, 'Pro-Boerism in Galway', 23 December 1899; National Library of Ireland Archives, Box 2, Folder 7; *World Book Encyclopaedia*, 'Boer', pp. 345.

3 – CONTRIBUTION TO THE GAELIC REVIVAL

1. Coogan, T. P. (1993) *De Valera: Long Fellow, Long Shadow*, p. 50; Crealey, *An Irish Almanac*, pp. 102, 112; Hodges, M. (1987) *Ireland, from Easter Uprising to Civil War*, pp. 13–14; O'Neill, *Wine and Gold*, pp. 25–6; National Library of Ireland Archives, Box 1, Folder 25 and Éamonn Ceannt, P2283.

2. Allen Library Archives, Box 198, File A, PKK 6, Letter from the General Post Office to Éamonn Ceannt 31 July 1905; Gallagher Family Manuscripts, Statement by Áine B. E. Ceannt, Inis

Ealga, Dundrum, County Dublin, Part II, 'Period from 1905 up to and including the Rising of Easter Week, 1916'; Hodges, *Ireland, from Easter Uprising to Civil War*, pp. 13–14; O'Neill, *Wine and Gold*, pp. 25–6; National Library of Ireland Archives, Box 2, Folder 7, 8, 19 and Éamonn Ceannt, P2283; *The Catholic Bulletin and Book Review*, 'Events of Easter Week: Biographies', Vol. VI, No. 7, July 1916, p. 396.

3. Allen Library Archives, Cumann na bPíobairí Minute Book 1900–04; O'Neill, *Wine and Gold*, pp. 25–6; RTÉ Archives, 'On Behalf of the Provisional Government' and 'Portraits 1916'; National Library of Ireland Archives, Box 2, Folder 7, 8 and Éamonn Ceannt, P2283.

4. Allen Library Archives, Cumann na bPíobairí Minute Book 1900–04; *Galway Advertiser*, 'Galway's Piping Tradition', 30 May 1991; Gallagher Family Manuscripts, Statement by Áine B. E. Ceannt, Inis Ealga, Dundrum, County Dublin, Part I, 'Autobiography of Áine B. E. Ceannt'; *The Catholic Bulletin and Book Review*, 'Events of Easter Week: Biographies', Vol. VI, No. 7, July 1916, p. 396; National Library of Ireland Archives, Box 2, Folder 7, 8; National Library of Ireland Archives, Cumann na bPíobairí Pipers Club Letter, MSS 13,069, 13,070.

5. The National Library of Ireland Archives: Éamonn Ceannt, (Miscellaneous Items), PC 166-666, Box 2 Folder 7, 8.

6. *The Pioneer*, September 1948, pp. 7–8.

4 – FALLING IN LOVE

1. Gallagher Family Manuscripts, Statement by Áine B. E. Ceannt, Part I; *The Catholic Bulletin and Book Review*, 'Events of Easter Week: Suffer the Little Children to Come Unto Me', Vol. VI, December 1916, p. 703; National Library of Ireland Archives, Box 4, Folder 7, Box 6, Folder 2 and Box 11, Dollard Book I.

2. Allen Library Archives, 'Éamonn Ceannt 1881–1916', Broadcast, P. Ó Congaile, 8 May 1942, Box 181, File 7; Gallagher Family

Manuscripts, Statement by Áine B. E. Ceannt, Part I; O'Neill, *Wine and Gold*, pp. 25–6; National Library of Ireland Archives, Box 1, Folder 25, Box 2, Folder 6 and Box 5, Folder 1.

3. Gallagher Family Manuscripts, Statement by Áine B. E. Ceannt, Part I; O'Neill, *Wine and Gold*, pp. 25–6; National Library of Ireland Archives, Box 2, Folder 6, 19.

4. Gallagher Family Manuscripts, 'Éamonn Ceannt' by Lily O'Brennan; Moira Kent Manuscripts, 'Account of Éamonn Ceannt', by Richard Ceannt; National Library of Ireland Archives, Box 1, Folder 25, Box 2, Folder 7, 8, 19.

5. Allen Library Archives, , Box 181, File 7, 'Éamonn Ceannt 1881–1916', Broadcast, P. Ó Congaile, 8 May 1942; RTÉ Archives, 'On Behalf of the Provisional Government' and 'Portraits 1916'; National Library of Ireland Archives, Éamonn Ceannt, IR94109.

6. Gallagher Family Manuscripts, Statement by Áine B. E. Ceannt, Part I and 'Kent family profile' by Joan and Mary Gallagher; Moira Kent Manuscripts, 'Account of Éamonn Ceannt' by Richard Ceannt; O'Neill, *Wine and Gold*, pp. 25–6; RTÉ Archives, 'On Behalf of the Provisional Government' and 'Portraits 1916'; St James's Church Parish Records, Certificate of Marriage; *The Catholic Bulletin and Book Review*, 'Events of Easter Week: Biographies', Vol. VI, No. 7, July 1916, p. 396.

7. Allen Library Archives, 'Éamonn Ceannt 1881–1916', Broadcast, P. Ó Congaile, 8 May 1942, Box 181, File 7; Boylan, H. (1998) *A Dictionary of Irish Biography*; Gallagher Family Manuscripts, Statement by Áine B. E. Ceannt, Part I; O'Neill, *Wine and Gold*, pp. 25–6; RTÉ Archives, 'On Behalf of the Provisional Government' and 'Portraits 1916'; National Library of Ireland Archives, Box 1, Folder 25, Box 2, Folder 6, 19 and Éamonn Ceannt, P2283.

8. *An Píobaire*, Vol. III, No. 11, July 1992; Allen Library Archives, Box 201, File B, PILT C, Postcard from Éamonn Ceannt in Rome to Alderman Tom Kelly, 30 September 1908, and Box 198, File A,

PKC 2, Postcard from Éamonn Ceannt in Rome to Áine Ceannt, 24 September 1908; National Museum of Ireland Archives, A1-95-007; *The Catholic Bulletin and Book Review*, 'Events of Easter Week: Suffer the Little Children to Come Unto Me', Vol. VI, December 1916, p. 703; National Library of Ireland Archives, Box 7, Folder 9.

5 – PATH TO REBELLION

1. Crealey, *An Irish Almanac*, p. 98; Davis, A. (1976) *Arthur Griffith*, pp. 4, 43; RTÉ Archives, television documentary, 19 November 2003, 'Hidden History'; National Library of Ireland Archives, Éamonn Ceannt, P2282.

2. Allen Library Archives, Box 181, File 7, 'Éamonn Ceannt 1881–1916', Broadcast, P. Ó Congaile, 8 May 1942; Dublin City Archives, 'Éamonn Ceannt and his employment history in Dublin Corporation' by Grainne Doran, 22 May 1995; Moira Kent Manuscripts, 'Account of Éamonn Ceannt' by Richard Ceannt; O'Neill, *Wine and Gold*, pp. 25–6; National Library of Ireland Archives, Box, 1, Folder 25, Box 2, Folder 19, MSS 13,069, 13,070.

3. Caulfield, M. (1995) *The Easter Rebellion*, p. 188; Collins, L. and Kostick, C. (2001) *The Easter Rising, A Guide to Dublin in 1916*, pp. 12–13; Crealey, *An Irish Almanac*; Dudley Edwards, R. (1990) *Patrick Pearse: The Triumph of Failure*, p. 155; Gallagher Family Manuscripts, Statement by Áine B. E. Ceannt, Part II; *Ireland's Eye*, July 2000; O'Toole, F. (1999) *The Irish Times Book of the Century*, pp. 29–30.

4. Crealey, *An Irish Almanac*, pp. 62, 117; Dudley Edwards, *Patrick Pearse*, pp. 157–9; Gallagher Family Manuscripts, Statement by Áine B. E. Ceannt, Part II; Hodges, *Ireland, from Easter Uprising to Civil War*; O'Neill, *Wine and Gold*, pp. 25–6; Preston, C. (n.d.) *A School History of Ireland, Part II, 1607–1949*, pp. 120–1; National Library of Ireland Archives, Box 2, Folder 8.

5. Crealey, *An Irish Almanac*, p. 40; Dudley Edwards, *Patrick Pearse*,

p. 180; Forester, M. (1972) *Michael Collins, The Lost Leader*, pp. 26–7; Moira Kent Manuscripts, 'Account of Éamonn Ceannt' by Richard Ceannt; O'Neill, *Wine and Gold*, pp. 25–6; Gallagher Family Manuscripts, Statement by Áine B. E. Ceannt, Part II and 'Kent family profile' by Joan and Mary Gallagher; *The Irish Press*, 'Éamonn Ceannt, fighting to the finish', 22 September 1981.

6. Caulfield, *The Easter Rebellion*, p. 16; Crealey, *An Irish Almanac*, p. 21.
7. Dirrane, B. (1997) *A Woman of Aran*, pp. 26–7; National Library of Ireland Archives, Éamonn Ceannt Address Book, MS 4733.

6 – FOUNDATION OF THE IRISH VOLUNTEERS

1. Allen Library Archives, Box 181, Volunteer Membership Card; Caulfield, *The Easter Rebellion*, p. 16; Crealey, *An Irish Almanac*, p. 151; Dudley Edwards, *Patrick Pearse*, p. 178; Gallagher Family Manuscripts, Statement by Áine B. E. Ceannt, Part II; Hodges, *Ireland, from Easter Uprising to Civil War*, p. 16.
2. Crealey, *An Irish Almanac*, p. 148; Hodges, *Ireland, from Easter Uprising to Civil War*, pp. 27–8; RTÉ Archives, 'On Behalf of the Provisional Government' and 'Portraits 1916'; National Library of Ireland Archives, Éamonn Ceannt, MS 2283; *Volunteer Gazette*, Christmas 1913.
3. Dudley Edwards, *Patrick Pearse*, pp. 208–9; Forester, *Michael Collins*, p. 29.
4. Dudley Edwards, *Patrick Pearse*, pp. 208, 210–11; Gallagher Family Manuscripts, Statement by Áine B. E. Ceannt, Part II.
5. Clarke, K. (1997) *Revolutionary Woman: My Fight for Ireland's Freedom*, p. 45; Gallagher Family Manuscripts, Statement by Áine B. E. Ceannt, Part I; McCoole, S. (1997) *Guns & Chiffon: Women Revolutionaries and Kilmainham Gaol, 1916–1923*, p. 13.

7 – Gun-Running

1. Coogan, *De Valera*, p. 54; Dudley Edwards, *Patrick Pearse*, pp. 214–217; Foster, *The Oxford Illustrated History of Ireland*, p. 233; Martin, F. X. (1964) *The Howth Gun-Running and the Kilcoole Gun-Running*, p. 136; Gallagher Family Manuscripts, Statement by Áine B. E. Ceannt, Part II; National Library of Ireland Archives, Éamonn Ceannt, MS 8838.

2. Dudley Edwards, *Patrick Pearse*, p. 237; Forester, *Michael Collins*, p. 355; Foster, *The Oxford Illustrated History of Ireland*, p. 233; RTÉ Archives, 'On Behalf of the Provisional Government' and 'Portraits 1916'.

3. Caulfield, *The Easter Rebellion*, pp. 17–18; Castleden, R. (1994) *British History: A Chronological Dictionary of Dates*, p. 295; Dudley Edwards, *Patrick Pearse*, pp. 221–2; Forester, *Michael Collins*, p. 130; National Library of Ireland Archives, Éamonn Ceannt, MS 10,883.

4. Caulfield, *The Easter Rebellion*, p. 18; Dudley Edwards, *Patrick Pearse*, pp. 217–26.

5. National Library of Ireland Archives, Éamonn Ceannt, MSS 13,069, 13,070.

8 – Planning for Rebellion

1. 'The Fourth Battalion', *Dublin Brigade Review*, 1939, p. 36; *Dublin's Fighting Story*, 'The South Dublin Union', *The Kerryman*, 1948, p. 31; Dudley Edwards, *Patrick Pearse*, p. 228; *Spark*, 7 and 28 March 1915; National Library of Ireland Archives, Éamonn Ceannt, MS 8286.

2. Allen Library Archives, Irish Volunteer Post, Box 181; Dudley Edwards, *Patrick Pearse*, pp. 240, 242; Gallagher Family Manuscripts, Statement by Áine B. E. Ceannt, Part II; National Library of Ireland Archives, Éamonn Ceannt MS 4733, MS 8286.

3. Dudley Edwards, *Patrick Pearse*, pp. 235–8, 242, 246.

4. Allen Library Archives, 'Éamonn Ceannt 1881–1916' by Donagh McDonagh, Box 181.

5. Caulfield, *The Easter Rebellion*, p. 18; Dudley Edwards, *Patrick Pearse*, pp. 246–7; Forester, *Michael Collins*, p. 34; Gallagher Family Manuscripts, Statement by Áine B. E. Ceannt, Part II.

6. Crealey, *An Irish Almanac*, p. 116; 'The Fourth Battalion', *Dublin Brigade Review*, 1939, p. 35; *Dublin's Fighting Story*, 'The South Dublin Union', *The Kerryman*, 1948, p. 32; Dudley Edwards, *Patrick Pearse*, p. 247; Forester, *Michael Collins*, pp. 34, 38–9, 355; Gallagher Family Manuscripts, Statement by Áine B. E. Ceannt, Part II.

7. Gallagher Family Manuscripts, Statement by Áine B. E. Ceannt, Part II; National Library of Ireland Archives, Éamonn Ceannt, IR94109.

8. Dudley Edwards, *Patrick Pearse*, p. 267; Gallagher Family Manuscripts, Statement by Áine B. E. Ceannt, Part II; *Galway Advertiser*, 'Recalling Liam Mellows, A little known episode', 28 March 1991, and 'Liam Mellows, On the Run in South Galway', 28 March 1996; Greaves, D. C. (1971) *Liam Mellows and the Irish Revolution*, pp. 81–2.

9 – HOLY WEEK

1. Allen Library Archives, invitation to ceilidhe, Box 201; Gallagher Family Manuscripts, Statement by Áine B. E. Ceannt, Part II.

2. Crealey, *An Irish Almanac*, p. 62; Gallagher Family Manuscripts, Statement by Áine B. E. Ceannt, Part II.

3. Caulfield, *The Easter Rebellion*, p. 21; Gallagher Family Manuscripts, Statement by Áine B. E. Ceannt, Part II.

4. Caulfield, *The Easter Rebellion*, pp. 33–4, 38; Collins and Kostick, *The Easter Rising*, p. 34; RTÉ Archives, 'On Behalf of the Provisional Government' and 'Portraits 1916'.

5. Caulfield, *The Easter Rebellion*, pp. 33, 36–7; Collins and Kostick, *The Easter Rising*, p. 34; Dudley Edwards, *Patrick Pearse*, p. 271;

Gallagher Family Manuscripts, Statement by Áine B. E. Ceannt, Part II.

10 – Mobilisation

1. Caulfield, *The Easter Rebellion*, p. 41; Collins and Kostick, *The Easter Rising*, p. 35; Davis, A. (1976) *Arthur Griffith*, p. 19; Gallagher Family Manuscripts, Statement by Áine B. E. Ceannt, Part II; *Sunday Independent*, 23 April 1916.
2. Collins and Kostick, *The Easter Rising*, p. 42; Extracts from the diary of Michael Kent; Gallagher Family Manuscripts, Statement by Áine B. E. Ceannt, Part II; RTÉ Archives, 'On Behalf of the Provisional Government' and 'Portraits 1916'.
3. Gallagher Family Manuscripts, Statement by Áine B. E. Ceannt, Part II.
4. Allen Library Archives, message from James Connolly, Box 105; Gallagher Family Manuscripts, Statement by Áine B. E. Ceannt, Part II.
5. Extracts from the diary of Michael Kent; Gallagher Family Manuscripts, Statement by Áine B. E. Ceannt, Part II.
6. Gallagher Family Manuscripts, Statement by Áine B. E. Ceannt, Part II; RTÉ Archives, 'On Behalf of the Provisional Government' and 'Portraits 1916'.
7. Allen Library Archives, messages from Cathal Brugha, Box 115, File A, 1; Caulfield, *The Easter Rebellion*, pp. 46–7; Gallagher Family Manuscripts, Statement by Áine B. E. Ceannt, Part II; *Irish Independent*, 'Parades Suddenly Cancelled', 24 April 1916.
8. Gallagher Family Manuscripts, Statement by Áine B. E. Ceannt, Part II; RTÉ Archives, 'On Behalf of the Provisional Government' and 'Portraits 1916'.
9. Gallagher Family Manuscripts, Statement by Áine B. E. Ceannt, Part II.
10. Gallagher Family Manuscripts, Statement by Áine B. E. Ceannt,

Part II; *Irish Independent*, 'A Licensed House Seized', 26–29 April, 1–4 May, 1916.

11 – A TERRIBLE BEAUTY IS BORN

1. Caulfield, *The Easter Rebellion*, pp. 1, 2, 53–5; *Oidhreacht 1916–1966*. Oifig an tSolathair, Baile Átha Cliath, pp. 6–7.
2. 'The Fourth Battalion', *Dublin Brigade Review*, 1939, p. 36; Extracts from the diary of Michael Kent.
3. Caulfield, *The Easter Rebellion*, pp. 57, 66–7, 84, 209; Collins and Kostick, *The Easter Rising*, p. 78; *Oidhreacht 1916–1966*, pp. 6–7.
4. Caulfield, *The Easter Rebellion*, pp. 46, 49, 74; Collins and Kostick, *The Easter Rising*, p. 45; *Irish Independent*, 'The Phoenix Park Fort', 26–29 April, 1–4 May, 1916.
5. Extracts from the diary of Michael Kent.

12 – SECURING THE UNION

1. Caulfield, *The Easter Rebellion*, pp. 50–1; *The Catholic Bulletin and Book Review*, 'Events of Easter Week: The fighting in the South Dublin Area', Part 1, Vol. VIII, April 1918, p. 153; *The Irish Press*, 'Éamonn Ceannt, fighting to the finish', 22 September 1981.
2. Caulfield, *The Easter Rebellion*, pp. 50–1; *The Catholic Bulletin and Book Review*, 'Events of Easter Week: The fighting in the South Dublin Area', Part 1, Vol. VIII, April 1918, pp. 153–4.
3. Caulfield, *The Easter Rebellion*, p. 51; *The Catholic Bulletin and Book Review*, 'Events of Easter Week: The fighting in the South Dublin Area', Part 1, Vol. VIII, April 1918, pp. 153–4 and 'Events of Easter Week: The fighting in the South Dublin Area', Part 2, Vol. VIII, April 1918, pp. 205–6.
4. Caulfield, *The Easter Rebellion*, pp. 52–3; *The Catholic Bulletin and Book Review*, 'Events of Easter Week: The fighting in the South Dublin Area', Part 1, Vol. VIII, April 1918, p. 156.

5. Caulfield, *The Easter Rebellion*, p. 52; Collins, S. (1996) *The Cosgrave Legacy*, p. 10; *The Catholic Bulletin and Book Review*, 'Events of Easter Week: The fighting in the South Dublin Area', Part 1, Vol. VIII, April 1918, pp. 154–6.

13 – ATTACK ON THE UNION

1. Caulfield, *The Easter Rebellion*, pp. 76–7; *The Catholic Bulletin and Book Review*, 'Events of Easter Week: The fighting in the South Dublin Area', Part 2, Vol. VIII, April 1918, p. 205.
2. Caulfield, *The Easter Rebellion*, pp. 77–8.
3. Caulfield, *The Easter Rebellion*, pp. 78–9, 92; *The Catholic Bulletin and Book Review*, 'Events of Easter Week: The fighting in the South Dublin Area', Part 2, Vol. VIII, April 1918, p. 207.
4. Caulfield, *The Easter Rebellion*, pp. 79–80; *The Catholic Bulletin and Book Review*, 'Events of Easter Week: The fighting in the South Dublin Area', Part 2, Vol. VIII, April 1918, p. 206.
5. Caulfield, *The Easter Rebellion*, p. 80; *The Catholic Bulletin and Book Review*, 'Events of Easter Week: The fighting in the South Dublin Area', Part 2, Vol. VIII, April 1918, pp. 206–8.
6. Caulfield, *The Easter Rebellion*, pp. 92, 93; *The Catholic Bulletin and Book Review*, 'Events of Easter Week: The fighting in the South Dublin Area', Part 3, Vol. VIII, May 1918, p. 257.
7. Caulfield, *The Easter Rebellion*, p. 93; *The Catholic Bulletin and Book Review*, 'Events of Easter Week: The fighting in the South Dublin Area', Part 3, Vol. VIII, May 1918, pp. 258–9.
8. Caulfield, *The Easter Rebellion*, pp. 93, 106–7.
9. Caulfield, *The Easter Rebellion*, pp. 106–7; Collins, *The Cosgrave Legacy*, p. 10; Gallagher Family Manuscripts, Statement by Áine B. E. Ceannt, Inis Ealga, Dundrum, County Dublin, Part III, 'The surrender as told by Miss Lily O'Brennan'; RTÉ Archives, 'On Behalf of the Provisional Government' and 'Portraits 1916'; *The Catholic Bulletin and Book Review*, 'Events of Easter Week', Part

2, Vol. VIII, April 1918, p. 208, and 'Events of Easter Week: The fighting in the South Dublin Area', Part 3, Vol. VIII, May 1918, pp. 259–60; National Library of Ireland Archives, Éamonn Ceannt (Miscellaneous Items), PC 166–666, Box 2, Folder 19.

10. Caulfield, *The Easter Rebellion*, pp. 105–6; RTÉ Archives, 'On Behalf of the Provisional Government' and 'Portraits 1916'; *The Catholic Bulletin and Book Review*, 'Events of Easter Week: The fighting in the South Dublin Area', Part 3, Vol. VIII, May 1918, pp. 259–60; National Library of Ireland Archives, Éamonn Ceannt (Miscellaneous Items), PC 166–666, Box 1, Folder 28, and Box 2, Folder 19.

14 – CALM BEFORE THE STORM

1. Caulfield, *The Easter Rebellion*, pp. 140, 142; Collins, *The Cosgrave Legacy*, p. 11; Crealey, *An Irish Almanac*, p. 58; 'The Fourth Battalion', *Dublin Brigade Review*, 1939, p. 36; *Dublin's Fighting Story*, 'The South Dublin Union', *The Kerryman*, 1948, p. 35; *The Catholic Bulletin and Book Review*, 'Events of Easter Week: The fighting in the South Dublin Area', Part 3, Vol. VIII, May 1918, pp. 259–60; National Library of Ireland Archives, Éamonn Ceannt (Miscellaneous Items), PC 166–666, Box 1, Folder 28; Vane, F. (1929) *Agin the Government: Memories and Adventures of Sir Francis Fletcher Vane, BT*, p. 263.

2. Extracts from the diary of Michael Kent; National Library of Ireland Archives, Éamonn Ceannt (Miscellaneous Items), PC 166–666, Box 1, Folder 28, and Éamonn Ceannt, MS 21,282.

3. Carty, J. (1966) *Ireland from The Great Famine to the Treaty of 1921: A Documentary Record*, p. 164; Collins and Kostick, *The Easter Rising*, pp. 12–13; *The Catholic Bulletin and Book Review*, 'Events of Easter Week: The fighting in the South Dublin Area', Part 4, Vol. VIII, May 1918, p. 309; *Irish Independent*, ' Liberty Hall Smashed', 26–29 April, 1–4 May, 1916; National Library of Ireland Archives, Éamonn

Ceannt, (Miscellaneous Items), PC 166–666, Box 1, Folder 28; Vane, *Agin the Government*, pp. 261, 270.

4. Gallagher Family Manuscripts, Statement by Áine B. E. Ceannt, Part II.

5. Extracts from the diary of Michael Kent; *Irish Independent*, 'Quietness Restored', 26–29 April, 1–4 May 1916.

15 – FINAL ASSAULT

1. Caulfield, *The Easter Rebellion*, pp. 220–2, 225; Coakley, D. and O'Doherty, M. (2002) *Borderlands: Essays on Literature and Medicine*, pp. 92, 96; *Dublin's Fighting Story*, 'The South Dublin Union', *The Kerryman*, 1948, p. 35; *The Catholic Bulletin and Book Review*, 'Events of Easter Week: The fighting in the South Dublin Area', Part 4, Vol. VIII, May 1918, p. 309.

2. Caulfield, *The Easter Rebellion*, pp. 223–4, 226–7; Collins, *The Cosgrave Legacy*, p. 11; *Dublin's Fighting Story*, 'The South Dublin Union', *The Kerryman*, 1948, p. 35; *The Catholic Bulletin and Book Review*, 'Events of Easter Week: The fighting in the South Dublin Area', Part 4, Vol. VIII, May 1918, p. 312.

3. Caulfield, *The Easter Rebellion*, pp. 227–30; Collins, *The Cosgrave Legacy*, p. 11; *The Catholic Bulletin and Book Review*, 'Events of Easter Week: The fighting in the South Dublin Area', Part 4, Vol. VIII, May 1918, p. 312; National Library of Ireland Archives, Éamonn Ceannt (Miscellaneous Items), PC 166–666, Box 2, Folder 19.

4. Caulfield, *The Easter Rebellion*, pp. 227–30; Coakley and O'Doherty, *Borderlands*, p. 97; Collins, *The Cosgrave Legacy*, p. 11; *The Catholic Bulletin and Book Review*, 'Events of Easter Week: The fighting in the South Dublin Area', Part 4, Vol. VIII, May 1918, p. 312.

16 – THE GALWAY REBELLION

1. Greaves, *Liam Mellows and the Irish Revolution*, pp. 84–6; *The*

Connacht Tribune, 'Galway 1916, Trustful Friends', 14 May 1966.

2. Collins, T., 'The *Helga/Muirchu*, her Contribution to Galway Maritime History', *Journal of the Galway Archaeological and Historical Society*, Vol. 52, 2002, pp. 150–2; Crealey, *An Irish Almanac*, p. 12; Dudley Edwards, *Patrick Pearse*, p. 295; *Galway Advertiser*, 'Liam Mellows, On the Run in South Galway', 28 March 1996; Greaves, *Liam Mellows*, pp. 87, 89; Interview, Kitty Lardner, 6 December 2003; *The Freeman's Journal*, 'Scenes in Galway, Three Professors Arrested', 6 May 1916.

3. Greaves, *Liam Mellows*, pp. 89–90; *The Connacht Tribune*, 'Galway 1916, Trustful Friends', 14 May 1966.

4. Greaves, *Liam Mellows*, pp. 89–94.

5. *Galway Advertiser*, 'Liam Mellows, On the Run in South Galway', 28 March 1996; Greaves, *Liam Mellows*, pp. 94, 99, 100–1.

17 – SURRENDER

1. Caulfield, *The Easter Rebellion*, pp. 221, 225; RTÉ Archives, 'On Behalf of the Provisional Government' and 'Portraits 1916'; *The Catholic Bulletin and Book Review*, 'Events of Easter Week: The fighting in the South Dublin Area', Part I, Vol. VIII, April 1918, p. 154.

2. Caulfield, *The Easter Rebellion*, p. 251; *The Catholic Bulletin and Book Review*, 'Events of Easter Week: The fighting in the South Dublin Area', Part 4, Vol. VIII, May 1918, p. 312; National Library of Ireland Archives, Éamonn Ceannt (Miscellaneous Items), PC 166–666, Box 1, Folder 28.

3. Gallagher Family Manuscripts, Statement by Áine B. E. Ceannt, Part II.

4. Caulfield, *The Easter Rebellion*, pp. 262, 273; *Oidhreacht 1916–1966*, p. 10; *The Irish Press*, 'With Cathal Brugha', 21 April 1933.

5. Caulfield, *The Easter Rebellion*, pp. 274–5; Dudley Edwards, *Patrick Pearse*, p. 307; Lee, J. (1989), *The Modernisation of Irish Society 1848–*

    1918, p. 156; *Oidhreacht 1916–1966*, p. 10; *The Irish Press*, 'Elizabeth
O'Farrell, Envoy of the Republic, the Last Day of the Rising', 22
April 1933.

6. Caulfield, *The Easter Rebellion*, p. 280; *The Irish Press*, 'Elizabeth
O'Farrell, Envoy of the Republic, the Last Day of the Rising', 22
April 1933.

7. Gallagher Family Manuscripts, Statement by Áine B. E. Ceannt,
Part II.

8. Mac Lochlainn, P. F. (1990) *Last Words*, pp. 129, 131; RTÉ Archives,
'On Behalf of the Provisional Government' and 'Portraits 1916';
National Library of Ireland Archives, Éamonn Ceannt (Miscellaneous
Items), PC 166–666, Box 1, Folder 29, and Box 2, Folder 19.

9. MacThomais, Éamonn, 'The South Dublin Union', *Dublin History
Review*, Vol. XXVI, 2 March 1973, p. 60; Gallagher Family
Manuscripts, Statement by Áine B. E. Ceannt, Part III; Mac
Lochlainn, *Last Words*, pp. 129, 131; RTÉ Archives, 'On Behalf of
the Provisional Government' and 'Portraits 1916'; National Library
of Ireland Archives, Éamonn Ceannt (Miscellaneous Items), PC
166–666, Box 1, Folder 28, and Box 2, Folder 19.

10. Gallagher Family Manuscripts, Statement by Áine B. E. Ceannt,
Part III; Mac Lochlainn, *Last Words*, p. 131.

11. Gallagher Family Manuscripts, Statement by Áine B. E. Ceannt,
Part III; Mac Lochlainn, *Last Words*, pp. 131–2, 143; National
Library of Ireland Archives, Éamonn Ceannt (Miscellaneous
Items), PC 166–666, Box 2, Folder 19.

18 – Court Martial

1. Mac Lochlainn, *Last Words*, p. 132; RTÉ Archives, 'On Behalf of
the Provisional Government' and 'Portraits 1916'; *The Irish Times*,
'List of Deported Prisoners', 11 May 1916; National Library of
Ireland Archives, Éamonn Ceannt (Miscellaneous Items), PC 166–
666, Box 1, Folder 28.

2. Extracts from the diary of Michael Kent; Gallagher Family Manuscripts, Statement by Áine B. E. Ceannt, Part II; *Irish Independent*, 'The New Commander', 26–29 April, 1–4 May, 1916; *The Irish Times*, 'The Arms Act', 3 May 1916, and 'Sir John Maxwell's Tribute', 11 May 1916.

3. British Military and Criminal History in the period 1900 to 1999, 'The 1916 Easter Uprising, Éamonn Ceannt', PRO (Public Records Office) Document WO 71/348; Crealey, *An Irish Almanac*, pp. 61–2; Extracts from the diary of Michael Kent; Gallagher Family Manuscripts, Statement by Áine B. E. Ceannt, Part II; Mac Lochlainn, *Last Words*, pp. 133–4.

4. British Military & Criminal History in the period 1900 to 1999, 'The 1916 Easter Uprising – Éamonn Ceannt', PRO Document WO 71/348.

5. British Military & Criminal History in the period 1900 to 1999, 'The 1916 Easter Uprising – Éamonn Ceannt', PRO Document WO 71/348.

6. Crealey, *An Irish Almanac*, p. 62; MacThomais, Éamonn, 'The South Dublin Union', *Dublin History Review*, Vol. XXVI, 2 March 1973, p. 60; Gallagher Family Manuscripts, Statement by Áine B. E. Ceannt, Part III; *The Freeman's Journal*, 'Death Sentences. Two Commuted to Life Terms. John McBride Shot', 6 May 1916; National Library of Ireland Archives, Éamonn Ceannt (Miscellaneous Items), PC 166–666, Box 1, Folder 23, and Éamonn Ceannt, MS 3198.

7. Gallagher Family Manuscripts, Statement by Áine B. E. Ceannt, Part II; Mac Lochlainn, *Last Words*, pp. 134–5.

19 – EXECUTION

1. Forester, *Michael Collins*, p. 60; Mac Lochlainn, *Last Words*, p. 139.

2. Mac Lochlainn, *Last Words*, pp. 136–7, 139–40; National Library of Ireland Archives, Éamonn Ceannt (Miscellaneous Items), PC 166–

666, Box 1, Folder 10, and Box 2, Folder 19, and Éamonn Ceannt, MS 18,556.

3. Gallagher Family Manuscripts, Statement by Áine B. E. Ceannt, Part II; Mac Lochlainn, *Last Words*, pp. 138–40.

4. Extracts from the diary of Michael Kent; Gallagher Family Manuscripts, Statement by Áine B. E. Ceannt, Part II; RTÉ Archives, 'On Behalf of the Provisional Government' and 'Portraits 1916'.

5. Extracts from the diary of Michael Kent; Gallagher Family Manuscripts, Statement by Áine B. E. Ceannt, Part II; Moira Kent Manuscript, 'Account of Éamonn Ceannt's last hours in Kilmainham' by Richard Ceannt.

6. Mac Lochlainn, *Last Words*, pp. 140–1.

7. Mac Lochlainn, *Last Words*, pp. 142–3

8. Extracts from the diary of Michael Kent; Gallagher Family Manuscripts, Statement by Áine B. E. Ceannt, Part II.

9. Gallagher Family Manuscripts, Statement by Áine B. E. Ceannt, Part II.

10. Mac Lochlainn, *Last Words*, p. 136.

20 – AFTERMATH

1. National Library of Ireland Archives, House of Commons letter to Áine Ceannt, MS 3198.

2. Gallagher Family Manuscripts, 'Éamonn Ceannt' by Lily O'Brennan; *The Connacht Tribune*, 'To Éamonn Ceannt', 8 May 1926; National Library of Ireland Archives, Éamonn Ceannt (Miscellaneous Items), PC 166–666, Box 1, Folder 10, and Éamonn Ceannt, IR 94109.

3. Caulfield, *The Easter Rebellion*, pp. 188, 288; Crealey, *An Irish Almanac*, pp. 34, 91, 104, 141, 157; Davis, *Arthur Griffith*, p. 19; Greaves, *Liam Mellows*, p. 221; Hodges, *Ireland, from Easter Uprising to Civil War*, pp. 17, 19–21, 34; Mac Lochlainn, *Last Words*, pp. 155–6, 193; Neeson, E. (1995) *The Civil War 1922–23*, p. 130.

4. *Irish Independent*, 'Sad Scenes at Glasnevin', 26–29 April, 1–4 May, 1916; *The Freeman's Journal*, 'Civilian Death Roll, 270 Accounted For, A Remarkable List; Dean's Grange Cemetery; Mount Jerome Cemetery', 12 May 1916.

5. Caulfield, *The Easter Rebellion*, p. 288; *The Irish Times*, 'Colonel Churchill's Suggestions', 11 May 1916.

6. Caulfield, *The Easter Rebellion*, p. 283.

7. 'The Fourth Battalion', *Dublin Brigade Review*, 1939, pp. 36–7; Hodges, *Ireland, from Easter Uprising to Civil War*, pp. 19, 30–1; *The Irish Times*, 'Prime Minister in Dublin', 14 May 1916; National Library of Ireland Archives, List of Irish Volunteers Killed Whilst Fighting For Ireland, MSS 13,069, 13,070.

EPILOGUE

1. Gallagher Family Manuscripts, Statement by Áine B. E. Ceannt, Part I and Part II; National Library of Ireland Archives, Éamonn Ceannt (Miscellaneous Items), PC 166–666, Box 1, Folder 19, Folder 23, Folder 28, and Box 4, Folder 7.

2. Gallagher Family Manuscripts, Statement by Áine B. E. Ceannt, Part I and Part II.

3. *Ibid*.

4. Foster, *The Oxford Illustrated History of Ireland*, p. 365; Gallagher Family Manuscripts, Statement by Áine B. E. Ceannt, Part I and Part II, and 'The Story of the Irish White Cross' by Áine Ceannt, p. 65; National Library of Ireland Archives, Éamonn Ceannt (Miscellaneous Items), PC 166–666, Box 1, Folder 23.

Bibliography

Boland, E. (1978) *W. B. Yeats and His World*, Thames and Hudson, London

Boylan, H. (1981) *Wolfe Tone*, Gill and Macmillan, Dublin

Boylan, H. (1998) *A Dictionary of Irish Biography*, Gill and Macmillan, Dublin

Carty, J. (1966) *Ireland from The Great Famine to the Treaty of 1921: A Documentary Record*, Fallon, Dublin

Castleden, R. (1994) *British History: A Chronological Dictionary of Dates*, Parragon Book Service, London

Caulfield, M. (1995) *The Easter Rebellion*, Gill and Macmillan, Dublin

Clarke, K. (1997) *Revolutionary Woman: My Fight for Ireland's Freedom*, O'Brien Press, Dublin

Collins, L. and Kostick, C. (2001) *The Easter Rising: A Guide to Dublin in 1916*, O'Brien Press, Dublin

Coakley, D. and O'Doherty, M. (2002) *Borderlands: Essays on Literature and Medicine*, Royal College of Surgeons, Dublin

Collins, S. (1996) *The Cosgrave Legacy*, Blackwater Press, Dublin

Coogan, T. P. (1990) *Michael Collins: A Biography*, Hutchinson, London

Coogan, T. P. (1993) *De Valera: Long Fellow, Long Shadow*, Hutchinson, London

Crealey, A.H. (1993) *An Irish Almanac*, Mercier Press, Cork

Davis, A. (1976) *Arthur Griffith*, Dundalgan Press, Dundalk

Dirrane, B. (1997) *A Woman of Aran*, Blackwater Press, Dublin

Dublin's Fighting Story, The Kerryman, 1948

Dudley Edwards, R. (1990) *Patrick Pearse: The Triumph of Failure*, Poolbeg Press, Dublin

Forester, M. (1972) *Michael Collins: The Lost Leader,* Sphere Books, London

Foster, R. F. (1989) *The Oxford Illustrated History of Ireland,* Oxford University Press, Oxford

Furey, B. (1991) *The History of Oranmore,* Brenda Furey, Maree

Greaves, D. C. (1971) *Liam Mellows and the Irish Revolution,* Lawrence and Wishart, London

Gregory, A. (1922) *70 Years 1852–1922,* Macmillan, New York

Harbison, P. (1992) *Guide to National and Historic Monuments of Ireland,* Gill and Macmillan, Dublin

Hayes-McCoy, G. A. (1990) *Irish Battles: A Military History of Ireland,* Appletree Press, Belfast

Hodges, M. (1987) *Ireland, from Easter Uprising to Civil War,* B. T. Batsford, London

Laffan, M. (1992) *Count Plunkett and his Times,* Foxrock Local History Club

Lee, J. (1989) *The Modernisation of Irish Society 1848–1918,* Gill and Macmillan, Dublin

Litton, H. (1994) *The Irish Famine, an Illustrated History,* Wolfhound Press, Dublin

Mac Lochlainn, P. F. (1990) *Last Words,* Government Publications, Dublin

Martin, F. X. (1964) *The Howth Gun-Running and the Kilcoole Gun-Running,* Brown and Nolan, Dublin

McCoole, S. (1997) *Guns and Chiffon: Women Revolutionaries and Kilmainham Gaol, 1916–1923,* Stationery Office, Dublin

Neeson, E. (1995) *The Civil War 1922–23,* Poolbeg Press, Dublin

O'Brien, P. (2010) *Uncommon Valour: 1916 and the South Dublin Union,* Mercier Press, Cork

Ó Faoláin, Seán (1980) *King of the Beggars: A Life of Daniel O'Connell,* Poolbeg Press, Dublin

O'Hara, B. (1984) *Michael Davitt Remembered,* The Michael Davitt National Memorial Association, Mayo

O'Toole, F. (1999) *The Irish Times Book of the Century*, Gill and Macmillan, Dublin

Preston, C. (n.d.) *A School History of Ireland, Part II, 1607–1949*, Browne and Nolan, Dublin

Shepherd, R. (1990) *Ireland's Fate: The Boyne and After*, Aurum Press, London

Shiel, M. and Roche, D. (eds) (1986) *A Forgotten Campaign, and Aspects of the Heritage of South-East Galway*, Woodford Heritage Group

Somerville-Large, P. (1995) *The Irish Country House, a Social History*, Sinclair-Stevenson, London

Vane, F. (1929) *Agin the Government: Memories and Adventures of Sir Francis Fletcher Vane, BT*, Samson Low, Marston and Co., London.

Woodham-Smith, C. (1962) *The Great Hunger*, Old Town Books, New York

PRIMARY SOURCES

Allen Library Archives

Dublin City Archives

Gallagher Family Manuscripts

Garda Archives

Kilmainham Gaol Archives

Michael Kent Diary

Moira Kent Manuscripts

National Library of Ireland Archives

National Museum of Ireland Archives

Public Records Office Archives, England

Radio Telefís Éireann (RTÉ) Archives

Registration of Births and Deaths in Ireland

Royal Irish Constabulary Register

St James's Church (Dublin) Archives

St James's Hospital Archives

William Kent Scroll

INTERVIEWS

Feeney, Andy, 'The 1900–01 Feis', 6 June 2000
Flaherty, Maura, 'Unveiling Plaque', 11 July 2001
Lardner, Kitty, 6 December 2003
McDonagh, Ann, 'Witness to Rebellion', 14 January 2001

SECONDARY SOURCES

Journals:
An Píobaire
Dublin Brigade Review
Dublin History Review
Journal of the Galway Archaeological and Historical Society
The Catholic Bulletin and Book Review

Magazines:
Ireland's Eye
The Pioneer
Spark
St Patrick's Parish Christmas Magazine
Volunteer Gazette
Wine and Gold 1966

Newspapers:
The Freeman's Journal
Galway Advertiser
The Galway Express
Irish Independent
The Irish Press
The Irish Times
The Limerick Leader

Booklets:

Kilmainham, The Kilmainham Jail Restoration Society, 1982

Oidhreacht 1916–1966, Oifig an tSolathair, Baile Átha Cliath

The Battle of Aughrim 1691, Interpretive Centre Booklet, Ireland West
    Tourism, Aras Fáilte, Galway

Reference Books:

O'Connor, Michael, *Scheduled History of the Dublin Pipers Club*

The Oxford Illustrated Dictionary, Second Edition, Book Club Associates,
    London, 1981

*To The Cause of Liberality: A history of the O'Connell Schools and the
    Christian Brothers, North Richmond Street*, FÁS, The Allen Library
    Project Committee, 1995

World Book Encyclopedia

Index

A

Albert, Fr 160
Aloysius, Fr 145, 149
Ancient Order of Hibernians 60
Arbour Hill Barracks 76
Ardee, Co. Louth 16, 28
Ardfert 83
Armstrong, Major J. A. 155–158
Asgard 61
Asquith, H. H. 51, 153, 180,
    184, 185
Athenry 68, 76, 136–138
Athlone 42, 126, 139
Aud 83, 84
Augustine, Fr 145, 149, 160,
    171–177

B

Bailey, Sgt Daniel 82, 83
Ballymoe 26, 27
Ballyporeen 26
Banda Rifle Club 53
Banna Strand 82
Barna 68
Barrett, Richard 183
Belfast 54, 124, 126
Blackader, Brigadier-General C.
    G. 155
Black Sea 47
Bloomsfield 54
Boer War 31, 32
Boland's Mills 101

Bowen-Colthurst, Capt. 124,
    125, 184
Boyd, Dr J. St Clair 35
Brugha, Cathal 88, 93, 94, 106,
    109, 111, 126, 131–133, 142,
    147, 160, 164, 183
Brugha, Mrs Kathleen 95, 96,
    127, 142, 145, 152, 160
Buachaillí na hÉireann 57
Burke, Frank 123, 186
Burke, Fr Thomas 139
Burke, Goban 121, 186

C

Cameron, Sir Charles 168
Carlow 184
Carnmore 138
Carson, Sir Edward 54, 55, 186
Casement, Roger 80, 82, 83, 85,
    182, 186
Castlegar 68, 137
Catholic Boys' Brigade 51
Ceannt, Áine (Frances Mary
    O'Brennan) 17, 41–45, 47,
    49, 52, 53, 57, 60, 71–73, 75,
    76, 78–81, 83–96, 125, 127,
    141, 142, 145, 148, 152, 153,
    155, 159–174, 176,–181,
    188–191
Ceannt, Rónán 17, 45, 71,
    79, 80, 93–95, 125, 127,
    159–161, 163, 165–167,
    171–174, 177, 179

Childers, Erskine 61
China 47
Clan na Gael 62, 74
Clanwilliam House 102
Claregalway 68, 137
Clarenbridge 137
Clarke, Kathleen 60
Clarke, Thomas 57, 63, 64, 67, 72, 73, 97, 143, 146, 154, 155, 186
Cleary, Ellen 26
Clifden 68
Clontarf 23, 36
Colbert, Con 106, 124, 147, 148, 165, 174, 186
College Green 75, 163
Collins, Michael 59, 74, 97, 144, 182
Connolly, James 58, 64, 72–74, 76, 89, 90, 97–99, 143, 144, 146, 182, 186
Connolly, Nora 76
Conscription Act 72
Corbett, Éamonn 135
Cork 26, 27, 83, 125, 168
Cosgrave, Phil 87
Cosgrave, William T. 111, 121, 131, 132, 134, 160, 183
Coughlan, James 121
Craughwell 137
Cregmore 137
Crofts, Joe 168
Cumann Cosanta, An 65
Cumann na bPíobairí (The Pipers' Club) 35, 36, 43
Cumann na mBan 55, 60, 124, 138, 147, 148, 150, 151, 188, 190, 191
Curragh, Co. Kildare 55, 108, 126

D

Dáil Éireann 15, 183
Dalkey 85, 86
Daly, Edward 66, 99, 100, 154, 186
Daly, Martin 39, 44, 75, 77, 181
Daly, Paddy 102
Davitt, Michael 24
Davys, Richard 156, 157
Dean's Grange Cemetery 184, 191
de Courcy Wheeler, Major 143
Derrydonnell 137
de Valera, Éamon 16, 66, 78, 101, 182
Devlin, Joseph 52
Devoy, John 74
Dickson, Thomas 125
Dillon, Fr 111
Dillon, Thomas 98
Dirrane, Bridget 55
Dolphin's Barn 72, 105
Dolphin Terrace 69, 95, 160
Donelan, Brendan 116, 187
Donovan, Con 151
Doyle, Crissie 168
Drogheda 28
Drumcondra (Dublin) 28, 100, 160, 161, 168
Dublin Castle 15, 73, 82, 99, 101, 152
Dublin Corporation 31, 48, 50, 80
Dublin Municipal Officers' Association 49
Dundalk 125

E

Emmet, Robert 19, 22, 42, 79, 188
Ennis, Martin 126

F

Fahy, Frank 77, 135
Fahy, Fr Thomas 139
Fahy, Pádraic 135
Fairview (Dublin) 28, 101
Famine 1845–47 23, 24
Fenian movement 24, 41, 53,
    70, 71
Fermoy 168
fFrench Mullen, Captain Doug-
    las 90, 132
Fianna Éireann 57, 124
Fianna Fáil 136
First World War 14
Fitzgibbon, Seán 49–51, 80, 81
Foley, Johnny 163
Four Courts 99, 100
Fourth Battalion 66, 69, 73–75,
    78, 89, 90, 93, 100, 105, 157,
    191
Furey, Terence 37

G

Gaelic League 16, 24, 33–35, 38,
    39, 42, 64
Galway 16, 24, 26, 27, 31, 35,
    37, 42, 43, 45, 55, 59, 68, 71,
    72, 76, 80, 93, 125, 135–138,
    176, 191
General Post Office (GPO) 97,
    98, 103, 104, 142, 191
Gerhard, Fr 111
German, Lieutenant-Colonel
    G. 155
Germany 63, 64, 74, 80, 82, 122,
    125, 126, 153, 185
Gibbon, Monk 129
Gifford, Grace 98, 155, 164
Glasnevin 70, 182, 184
Gregory, Lady 37

Griffith, Arthur 48, 54, 64, 85,
    98, 183

H

Hales, Seán 184
Helga, HMS 126
Heuston, Seán 100, 155, 165,
    174, 187
Hobson, Bulmer 62, 65, 81, 135
Home rule 14, 51, 52, 54, 55, 63,
    64, 186
Hospital 2–3, South Dublin
    Union 110, 116, 117, 119
Howley, Joseph 135, 137
Howley, Peadar 139
Howth 61, 62, 91
Hunter, Thomas 160
Hynes, Frank 139

I

Inghinidhe na hÉireann 60
Irish Citizen Army 58, 64, 73,
    97, 99, 101, 124, 126
Irish Nationalist Party 51, 52, 60
Irish Red Cross 191
Irish Republican Brotherhood
    (IRB) 20, 53, 58–60, 62–65,
    67, 72–74, 76, 81, 82, 88,
    121, 136
Irish Volunteer 152, 160
Irish Volunteers 20, 56–66, 68–72,
    74–76, 78, 80–85, 87, 88, 90,
    91, 93, 96, 97, 100–103, 105,
    106, 108–110, 112, 114–124,
    128, 130, 132, 135–140, 144,
    146–148, 150–153, 158, 163,
    170, 182, 183, 186
Irish White Cross 189
Irvine, George 78, 108, 110, 114,
    116, 117

Islandbridge Barracks 103, 108, 110

J

Jacob's Factory 101, 145, 156–158
Jameson's Distillery 106, 110, 115, 124, 129, 147
Joyce, John 110, 115, 120, 132, 133, 164

K

Keegan, Millie 92
Kehoe, Nurse 184
Kelly, Captain Roche 112
Kelly, Tom 47, 80
Kent, James (Ceannt's brother) 27, 44, 45
Kent, James (Ceannt's father) 16, 26–28
Kent, John P. (Ceannt's brother) 27, 167, 168
Kent, Lieutenant-Colonel W. J. 155
Kent, Michael (Ceannt's brother) 27, 86, 90, 91, 103, 104, 125, 127, 128, 152, 167, 169–171, 175, 179
Kent, Nell (Ceannt's sister) 27, 32, 90, 91, 100, 125, 128, 160, 163, 167, 168, 176, 177, 179
Kent, Richard (Ceannt's brother) 27, 86, 125, 161, 163, 167, 169–172, 177, 179
Kent, Thomas 169, 187
Kent, William (Ceannt's brother) 27, 31, 44, 45, 167–169, 188
Keogh, Nurse Margaret 119
Kilcoole, Co. Wicklow 62

Kilmainham Gaol 161, 163, 165–167, 169, 172, 176–178, 181
Kingsbridge (Heuston) station 50, 108
King's Own Scottish Borderers 62
Kinvara 139
Kirby, Rev. Dr Tobias 41, 42, 47

L

Land League 24
Lardner, Larry 135–137
Larkfield (Kimmage) 74
Larkin, James 58
Larne, Co. Antrim 61
Lea Wilson, Capt. 144
Liberty Hall 89, 90, 97, 126
London 60, 182
Lowe, Brigadier-General 143, 145

M

MacBride, John 64, 152, 156, 157, 160, 170, 187
MacCarthy, Capt. Thomas 106, 110
MacCarthy, Dan 92
Mac Diarmada, Seán 50, 53, 58, 63, 64, 67, 72, 73, 82, 97, 98, 143, 182, 187
MacDonagh, Thomas 50, 64, 66, 75, 78, 82, 88, 90, 99, 101, 145–147, 154–157, 187
MacDowell, William 121
MacEntee, Seán 136
Mac Giobúin, Seán 168
MacNeill, Eoin 33, 52, 56–58, 63–65, 75, 81, 82, 84, 85, 88, 89, 92, 93, 106, 135, 136, 182, 183

Maconchy, Brigadier-General E. W. S. 134

Mallin, Michael 101, 165, 174, 187

Malone, Lieut George 112, 113

Maree, Co. Galway 68, 137

Markievicz, Countess 101

Martyn, Capt. Mickey 129–131, 133, 134, 140

Martyn, Edward 34

Maxwell, General Sir John 102, 139, 153, 158, 159, 177, 185

McDonagh, Pat 36

McIntyre, Patrick 125

McKelvey, Joseph 184

Mellows, Barney 76, 77, 93

Mellows, Liam 57, 60, 75–77, 79, 93, 135–139, 183

Mellows, Mrs 76, 80, 87, 89, 168, 181

Mendicity Institution 100

Metropole Hotel 89

Milner, Major 113

Monncháin, Ailbhe Ó 139

Monteith, Robert 82, 85

Mount Brown 110–113, 115, 120, 123

Mount Jerome Cemetery 184

Mountjoy Jail 183

Mount Street Bridge 102

Moylan, Seán 13, 14

Murphy, Capt. Séamus 89, 106, 124, 148, 168

Murphy, William 58

N

National Volunteers 64

Neilan, Matthew 135

Nicholas, George 136, 138

Night Nurses' Home, South Dublin Union 111, 126, 129–132

Nolan, Mary 168

North Richmond Street 28, 31

O

Oates, Captain John 129–131, 133

Oates, Lieutenant-Colonel W. C. 129

O'Brennan, Lily 41, 43, 57, 60, 87, 91, 93, 148, 150, 161, 165, 167, 168, 181, 191

O'Brien, Constable James 99

O'Brien, William 64, 110, 115

Ó Conaire, Pádraic 60

O'Connell, Daniel 23, 28

O'Connor, Rory 183

O'Donovan Rossa, Jeremiah 70

O'Farrell, Nurse Elizabeth 143, 145, 150

O'Hanrahan, Michael 154, 187

O'Kelly, Seán T. 64

O'Leary, John 142

O'Rahilly, Michael Joseph (The O'Rahilly) 49, 50, 54, 56, 65, 84, 97, 98, 142, 187

Oranmore, Co. Galway 68, 136, 137

O'Reilly, Richard 116, 187

Owen, Colonel R. L. 112

Owens, John 113, 187

P

Parnell, Charles Stewart 29, 51, 144

Pearse, Margaret 79

Pearse, Mrs 79

Pearse, Patrick 15, 33, 50, 52, 55–58, 60, 63–65, 67, 70–72, 79, 81, 82, 84, 97–99, 121,

122, 135, 136, 142–144, 146,
154, 155, 187
Pearse, William 79, 154, 187
Penal Laws 21
Phoenix Park 29, 83, 93, 100,
102, 103
Píobaire, An 35
Plunkett, Count 189
Plunkett, Geraldine 98
Plunkett, Joseph Mary 55,
64–67, 72, 74, 89, 97, 98,
143, 154, 155, 164, 187
Portobello Barracks 96, 126, 129
Portobello Bridge 96
Post Gaelach, An 68, 69, 86

Q

Queenstown (Cobh) 83
Quinn, James 116, 187

R

Raftery, Anthony 37, 38
Ramsay, Lieutenant Alan 113,
114, 184
Reddin, Kerry 57
Redmond, John 52, 60, 63, 64,
186
Reilly, Martin 35, 36
Reynolds, George 102, 187
Rialto gate, North Dublin Union
105, 108, 110, 111, 113–116,
130
Rice, Edmund 28
Richmond Barracks 108–110,
148, 150, 151, 158, 159,
161–163
Rome 41, 42, 45–47
Royal Dublin Fusiliers 27, 45
Royal Hospital, Kilmainham
108, 113–115, 124, 129

Royal Irish Constabulary (RIC)
16, 26–28, 126, 136, 138

S

Sarsfield, Patrick 21
Second Battalion 101
Sheehy-Skeffington, Francis 124,
125, 184
Shelbourne Hotel 101
Sherwood Foresters 126, 153
Sinn Féin 24, 48, 49, 52, 54, 119,
183, 186, 189, 190
South Dublin Union 86, 105–
117, 121, 122, 124–127, 129,
130, 134, 140, 141, 145–149,
153, 159, 165, 184
Spiddal 45, 68, 71, 72
Spindler, Capt. Karl 83
St Enda's 79, 80, 81
Stephens, James 53
St Patrick's Park 157
St Stephen's Green 101, 144
Sweeney, Patrick 156, 157

T

Templemore 126
Third Royal Irish Regiment 112
Thornton, Michael 45, 71, 72
Tone, Theobald Wolfe 19, 20, 22,
50, 188
Tralee 81
Traynor, John 114, 187
Trinity College Dublin 50
Troup, Sir Edward 185
Tulla, Co. Clare 139

U

Uileann pipes 34
Ulster Unionists 54, 63

Ulster Volunteer Force (UVF)
    54, 61
United National Societies Com-
    mittee 49

V

Vane, Sir Francis 126, 129, 130,
    133, 134, 146, 147, 184
Vatican 42, 46

W

Walker, Sergeant 131
Warmington, Captain Edward
    113, 114
Waterford 27, 41
Watkin's Brewery 106, 124
Wellington Barracks 96
Whelan, Constable P. 138
Women's Hospital, South Dublin
    Union 115, 120
Wyse Power, Jenny 60

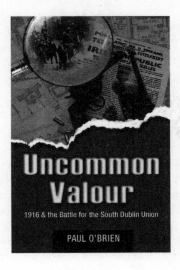

Uncommon Valour: 1916 & the Battle for the South Dublin Union

Paul O'Brien

978 1 85635 654 1

On Easter Monday, 1916, Éamonn Ceannt and 120 men of the 4th Battalion of the Irish Volunteers occupied the South Dublin Union, a workhouse and hospital spread over fifty-two acres near James's Street, Dublin. This was the beginning of a week-long bloody engagement with British crown forces as part of the 1916 Rising.

Uncommon Valour is a detailed account of the events that took place within the South Dublin Union which resulted in two major battles and a number of violent skirmishes. The beleaguered Irish Volunteers fought a desperate campaign against overwhelming odds to defend their newly declared Republic. Éamonn Ceannt and Cathal Brugha led the small group of Irish Volunteers who held off the might of the British army, surrendering only when ordered to by the Rising's leaders.

www.mercierpress.ie

MERCIER PRESS

IRISH PUBLISHER - IRISH STORY

We hope you enjoyed this book.

Since 1944, Mercier Press has published books that have been critically important to Irish life and culture. Books that dealt with subjects that informed readers about Irish scholars, Irish writers, Irish history and Ireland's rich heritage.

We believe in the importance of providing accessible histories and cultural books for all readers and all who are interested in Irish cultural life.

Our website is the best place to find out more information about Mercier, our books, authors, news and the best deals on a wide variety of books. Mercier tracks the best prices for our books online and we seek to offer the best value to our customers, offering free delivery within Ireland.

Sign up on our website or complete and return the form below to receive updates and special offers.

www.mercierpress.ie
www.facebook.com/mercier.press
www.twitter.com/irishpublisher

Name:

Email:

Address:

Mobile No.:

Mercier Press, Unit 3b, Oak House, Bessboro Rd, Blackrock, Cork, Ireland